My
Journey
with # Maya

ALSO BY TAVIS SMILEY

My Journey *with* Maya

TAVIS SMILEY
WITH DAVID RITZ

Little, Brown and Company

New York Boston London

Little, Brown and Company
Hachette Book Group
1290 Avenue of the Americas
New York, NY 10104
littlebrown.com

First Edition: April 2015

Little, Brown and Company is a division of Hachette Book Group, Inc. The Little, Brown name and logo are trademarks of Hachette Book Group, Inc.

The publisher is not responsible for websites (or their content) that are not owned by the publisher.

The Hachette Speakers Bureau provides a wide range of authors for speaking events. To find out more, go to hachettespeakersbureau.com or call (866) 376-6591.

Maya Angelou poems and excerpts used with permission of Caged Bird Legacy, LLC.

ISBN 978-0-316-34175-2

LCCN: 2015933793

10 9 8 7 6 5 4 3 2 1

RRD-C

Printed in the United States of America

For the mothers in my life:
Joyce Smiley, Daisy M. Robinson,
Adel Smiley, Eula Collins,
Irene West, Maya Angelou

Contents

Contents

My
Journey
with Maya

Prologue

Maya Angelou and I shared a friendship that I count as one of the great blessings of my life. As you will soon see, she appeared—and kept appearing—exactly when my spirit required repair. I do not consider those appearances coincidences but rather precious gifts.

The aim of this book is to share those gifts with you.

It's a lesson Maya Angelou taught me. Maya was all about sharing. In her writing and public appearances, her soaring spirit attracted legions of loyal fans. But without minimizing those literary and televised encounters, I have to say that the personal experience—the one-on-one, face-to-face meeting with Maya—held a power all its own. Those are the meetings, whether during our journey to Africa or in her homes in Harlem and North Carolina, that I seek to bring to life in this memoir.

I do so to honor my dear friend and, to the best of my ability, give you what she gave me—words and attitudes that invigorate the soul. Maya's great mission was to demonstrate how courageous love can heal even the deepest wounds. She taught me about bravery, about listening, about language.

The ideas expressed to me were ones she had shared—and would continue to share—with many others. She was remarkably consistent in expressing her loving vision and strategies for spiritual survival. Maya freely spread her sagacity to as many people as possible and in as many forms as possible. I was only one of many who had the good fortune to sit by her side and glean her wisdom.

When we met, I was in my twenties and Maya was in her late fifties, a strong and vital presence. During the course of our twenty-eight-year dialogue, we both faced enormous challenges and went through life-altering changes. Up close, I was privileged to see how Maya responded to those challenges and changes. And most poignantly, I was able to see how she approached what many consider the greatest trial of all: impending mortality.

Maya's immortality rests in the beautiful body of

work she left behind. Undoubtedly she will be discovered and rediscovered by generations to come. Just as Paul Robeson is remembered as the greatest Renaissance man in the history of black America—athlete, actor, activist, scholar, singer, lawyer—I believe Maya will be remembered as black America's greatest Renaissance woman—dancer, poet, actor, screenwriter, memoirist, director, lyricist, activist.

A brief note about the form of this book:

Maya Angelou was blessed with an extraordinary voice. By quoting her, I strive to convey the haunting beauty and lilting musicality of her storytelling. She told and retold many stories, some of which you'll read here; other conversations I recount were private and have never appeared anywhere else. In re-creating her voice for this text, I have based quotations on the copious notes I took during our private encounters, the transcripts of our many public conversations, my best recollections, and the complete written works of Maya Angelou.

I hope that by writing down for you Maya's impact on my life I can shed new light on her luminous character. I miss her every day, and if this book lets you see her, hear her, and feel her spirit, I will be gratified—satisfied that I have done what, in both word and deed, Maya urged us all to do:

Pass on the love.

PART ONE

The Motherland

I

Taking Off

My life was filled with purpose.

But nothing could have prepared me for what I was about to do. I had a letter to deliver to Maya Angelou. It was the early 1990s. In my senior year at Indiana University, I had sought out and miraculously persuaded Tom Bradley, the first black mayor in the history of Los Angeles, to hire me as one of his many assistants. It didn't matter that my job assignments were mundane—filling in for the mayor at low-level ribbon-cutting ceremonies, accompanying the mayor's wife to her medical appointments, writing countless administrative memos. I was thrilled to be working for a dedicated and powerful public servant.

Growing up in a trailer park in rural Indiana, a black kid in a white world, I had gravitated toward mentors and public servants such as Kokomo city councilman Douglas Hogan and Bloomington mayor Tomilea Allison. I liked the way they gave voice to the voiceless. I, too, wanted to champion the downtrodden. Martin Luther King Jr. was my spiritual and political hero, and I wanted to do all I could to right society's wrongs.

It wasn't until college that I had the chance to sit under the teachings of black instructors. In my first course in Afro-American studies, Professor Fred McElroy lectured on the subject of two women whose writing impressed me deeply—Toni Morrison and Maya Angelou. So when Ms. Morrison was scheduled to lecture at the university, I was the first to show up and take a seat in the front row. She spoke with rare eloquence. She spoke not only of the long and hallowed history of African American expression in literature, art, music, and dance but also touched upon European philosophy, Freudian psychology, and Greek mythology. Her intellectual discourse had me reeling. So eager was I to engage her in dialogue that the moment she invited questions, mine was the first hand to pop up. I asked her about her career—certainly nothing profound. I just wanted to be part of the discussion.

I couldn't blame Ms. Morrison for summarily dismissing me. She rolled her eyes, sighed, and gave a short, curt response. Her disdain was understandable. If I didn't have a real question to ask, why bother? Why waste her time and the time of this assembly?

I had no follow-up. I quickly retreated, searching for a hole in the floor through which to disappear.

That marked my first experience with a world-famous intellectual.

Several years passed. I was working in Los Angeles when Mayor Bradley asked me to bring a personal letter of welcome to Dr. Maya Angelou, who was appearing before a philanthropic organization. Given my experience with Toni Morrison, you can understand why I was extremely cautious in my approach, to the point of being intimidated.

I reminded myself that I was only a glorified errand boy. Just hand-deliver the letter and leave.

When I arrived, the program had not yet begun. I found Dr. Angelou seated in front of fifty or sixty people. Surrounded by many admirers, she exuded dignity and patience as, one by one, she greeted her fans and exchanged a few pleasantries.

Quite correctly, I said, "Dr. Angelou, it's my privilege to present you with this letter from our mayor. He regrets that urgent city business prevents him from being here in person."

"I understand, young man," she said. Her eye contact was intense and sustained. "You'll be certain to give the mayor my warmest regards."

"I certainly will."

The encounter ended there. For a second, I thought of telling her how much her memoirs meant to me; how deeply I loved her poetry; how I yearned to learn more about her relationship with Dr. King and Malcolm X. There were a million and one questions I yearned to ask. But knowing that this was neither the time nor the place, I turned and left. Besides, the mayor had me running to another event, which meant I couldn't even stay for the program.

I had brushed up against greatness, and even just that brief whisper of being near Maya left me burning to see her again.

Life went on.

I was working for a meager city salary, but my personality was much bigger than my earnings. Even though I was still unable to pay off my college loans, I was a young man on fire, determined to make my mark, to somehow make a difference.

The mayor, with his strong sense of public duty, was all about practicality. And although I considered him my champion, ours was purely a professional relationship.

Unlike me, he was not given to far-reaching discussions or intellectual probing.

Because he knew of my college background in debating, Mayor Bradley allowed me to give speeches on his behalf. He also named me as one of six area coordinators who were to help him oversee the city. We acted essentially as junior mayors. I became his eyes and ears in South Los Angeles. The point of the job was to diligently bring the needs of the citizens to the attention of the mayor, who increasingly trusted my judgment.

I was riding high when suddenly the rug was pulled out from under me. The mayor hired a new deputy mayor, a young white boy from Harvard, who promptly restructured the system of area coordinators. Within days I lost my office in Bradley's suite, my city car, and my secretary. I was relegated to the lowly office where, years earlier, I'd started out as an intern.

It took me a while to bring my complaint to the mayor, a man who disliked confrontations.

"I'll return a city car to you, Tavis," he said in his usual efficient manner, "but beyond that I won't undercut the authority of my deputy mayor."

I was stuck, unsure of what to do, until Magnificent Montague, a local DJ famous for the phrase "Burn, baby, burn!" told me in his big-brotherly way, "Don't fret, T. This is your chance to step out and do your own thing."

My own thing had been clear to me since high school: public service. What better way to serve the public than through elective office?

Because I had made a name for myself, I decided to run for a city council seat. I'd be up against a popular incumbent, but with my energy and commitment to an all-out campaign, I didn't see how I could lose.

Not only did I lose, I also failed to make the runoff. Friends consoled me by saying that, as a newcomer, I did well. But losing is losing, and I was down. As a competitor—and a fierce one, at that—I hit bottom. For all my burning ambition and grand plans, at twenty-six I was something of a lost soul.

Fortunately, friends rallied around me. A year or two earlier I had begun an organization of young black professionals through which I met Julianne Malveaux, a nationally syndicated columnist and economist who held a PhD from MIT. A brilliant woman, Julianne was a concerned friend. She saw that my defeat at the polls had taken its toll.

"What you need, Tavis, is a trip—something to get your mind off yourself."

"I wouldn't mind a trip," I said. "But to where?"

"How about going to Africa with Dr. Maya Angelou?"

*   *   *

"What are you talking about?" I asked Julianne. The idea was so out of nowhere that I had to hear her out. The charge of my first meeting with Maya, of her intensity and commitment to every moment, had never left me.

"Maya and I are close. We met through our mutual friend Ruth Love."

Dr. Ruth Love, who had been superintendent of school districts in Oakland and Chicago, was one of the country's leading educators.

"We're both accompanying Maya next month on a trip to Ghana. Ruth and I are speaking for the National Council for Black Studies, and Maya will be delivering a major address at the W. E. B. Du Bois Memorial Centre for Pan-African Culture. I'll be talking about the global economy with a focus on the United States' role in African development. Ruth will speak on education. Other scholars will be making presentations, including the great historian Dr. John Henrik Clarke."

I knew of Dr. Clarke—one of the pioneers in the field of black studies.

"I'm sure Maya would love to have you come along," said Julianne.

"What makes you so sure?"

"She thrives on meeting new people—especially intellectually curious young people."

"I'm not sure what I'd do on the trip."

"How about carrying her bags?"

"I'd be honored. But are you sure I'd be welcome?"

"Positive. This is a special trip for Maya. You might remember that she lived in the capital city, Accra. This will be something of a homecoming. You won't want to miss it."

Truth was, I knew I just had to go. I really couldn't afford it. The campaign had left me even deeper in debt than I had been before. And a round-trip ticket to Ghana cost a fortune. But when I mentioned that to Julianne, she surprised me.

"I have a ton of frequent-flyer miles, Tavis. We'll use those to get you a ticket. I might even have enough to get you into business class."

"Julianne, I'm flabbergasted, I really am. I don't know what to say."

"Just say yes."

I said yes.

"Now start reading up on Ghana."

Ghana! By the time I put down the phone, my despondency over the lost election was gone. I ran to the library—easy access to the Internet was years away—and voraciously consumed article after article about Ghana. I also reread large portions of Dr. Angelou's work, especially *All God's Children Need Traveling Shoes,* her fifth memoir, in which she recounts the years that she lived in Accra, Ghana's capital.

Situated in West Africa between Ivory Coast and Togo, Ghana—formerly the Gold Coast—was the first country in sub-Saharan Africa to gain independence. When Dr. Angelou moved there from Cairo in 1962, she was a thirty-four-year-old single mother with a college-age son, a woman wandering through the world on the strength of her inexhaustible spirit. Before Egypt, where she edited a newspaper, she had lived in New York and played the role of Queen in Jean Genet's avant-garde play *The Blacks.* In the cast were James Earl Jones, Louis Gossett Jr., and Cicely Tyson. She had been a member of the famed Harlem Writers Guild and performed *Cabaret for Freedom,* which she cowrote and coproduced with Godfrey Cambridge. Also known as Miss Calypso, she was a popular dancer and singer; she appeared at the Apollo, recorded an album of her own, and performed in the film *Calypso Heat Wave* with Alan Arkin and Joel Grey. She wasn't just sitting around.

In Accra, she was the center of an illustrious circle of expatriates, including Julian Mayfield, an actor, novelist, and activist. Living in exile, he became a writer for President Kwame Nkrumah, thought to be the most progressive and enlightened leader on the African continent.

It was Nkrumah who led Ghana to independence from British colonization, only five years before Dr. Angelou arrived in Accra.

From my reading about Martin Luther King Jr., I remembered that he—along with Ralph Bunche, Adam Clayton Powell Jr., A. Philip Randolph, publisher John H. Johnson, and Vice President Richard Nixon—had attended Nkrumah's inauguration in 1957. In fact, Nkrumah, who invited Dr. and Mrs. King to a private luncheon, was the first head of state to welcome the Baptist preacher.

And it was President Nkrumah who financed the ambitious *Encyclopedia Africana* project, which brought the man himself—W. E. B. Du Bois—to Ghana at the age of ninety-three. Two years later, when the American government, still intent on persecuting Du Bois for his left-leaning sympathies, refused to renew his passport, he became a Ghanaian citizen.

When Dr. Angelou arrived, Du Bois and his wife, Shirley, were still living in Accra. And just as exciting to my young imagination was the fact that it was in Ghana where Dr. Angelou spent a week with Malcolm X, who had come to Africa after his life-altering pilgrimage to Mecca.

Maya's trip was to take place in August of 1993. Only seven months earlier, Bill Clinton had requested that Dr. Angelou write and recite a poem on the occasion of his inauguration as president of the United States. Only one other poet—Robert Frost, at the inauguration of John Kennedy—had been so honored. In the long history of the august ceremony, Dr. Angelou was the first woman and first person of color to read verse. She and Clinton shared Arkansas roots—he came from the little town of Hope; she had spent much of her childhood in a rural village called Stamps.

When Dr. Angelou went to the podium and in the bright light of the winter sun recited "On the Pulse of Morning," a poem whose grand theme of radical inclusion conveyed a spirit of optimism with ringing clarity, millions of Americans leaned toward their televisions.

"The horizon leans forward," she read, "Offering you space to place new steps of change..../ Here, on the pulse of this new day / You may have the grace to look up and out / And into your sister's eyes, and into / Your brother's face, your country / And say simply / Very simply / With hope— / Good morning."

In that assembly of world leaders, her presence was commanding. She owned the moment. Her delivery was effortless, her eloquence underscored by the passion of her conviction. I marveled at the utter confidence with which she spoke.

* * *

In the days before leaving for Ghana, I had trouble falling asleep. This was my first time out of the country. Beyond that, though, I stayed awake with a strange feeling that it was all too good to be true; that somehow Julianne Malveaux and Ruth Love had been presumptuous in inviting me; and that at the last moment I'd be told that Dr. Angelou preferred not to introduce a stranger into her entourage.

But that didn't happen. Despite my fears, the trip was on.

Julianne, Ruth, and I were on the same flight. Dr. Angelou was to arrive the next day.

On the long trip overseas, I mainly tried to keep my cool. That wasn't easy. I felt like a little boy on the biggest adventure of his life. I wanted to jump out of my seat and shout, "The Motherland! I'm going to the Motherland!"

Instead of acting the fool, I spent most of the trip reading about Ghana, a country sometimes called an island of peace in a part of the world known for bloody conflict.

I started jotting down a list of questions I wanted to ask Dr. Angelou about her time in Ghana in the 1960s, a period that coincided with some of the headiest days of the American civil rights movement. How would she characterize President Nkrumah's relationship with Dr.

King? Did she and Malcolm discuss King? If so, what did Malcolm have to say about King? I knew that Dr. Angelou had worked closely with King; what was it like to be in his company? Thinking back over her long list of close friends—the illustrious people she wrote about in her memoirs—I realized there were dozens of questions I wanted to ask her about Richard Wright and Ralph Ellison, James Baldwin and Amiri Baraka, Nina Simone and Nikki Giovanni.

As the jumbo jet droned on through the night, my notes became more and more voluminous. I realized that Dr. Angelou was a link—a living link—to much of the contemporary black cultural history that I had studied in college. There were more than a million things to ask her. My mind was overwhelmed by curiosity.

Approaching the Accra airport at the end of the long flight, I had the good judgment to crumple up my notes and throw them away. I realized that this woman was not coming to Ghana to entertain my questions. She was returning to a country she loved to see old friends and deliver a lecture. Because she was a world-renowned figure and a former resident, the local press would surely be approaching her. After granting God knows how many interviews, the last thing she'd need was another interview conducted by a tagalong. I needed to remember that I had volunteered to assist her, to do what she needed, to carry her bags. I needed to stay humble. In all probability there'd be little or no private time with her. My job was to stay quiet, stay out of her way, and be helpful whenever the occasion arose.

Remember what happened with Toni Morrison, I reminded myself. *Don't play the fool. Don't go shooting off your mouth when you have nothing to say.*

Having given myself a stern lecture, I felt better. It was enough to simply experience the Motherland. That in and of itself was a gift. Anything beyond that would be gravy.

The plane landed with a thud.

Passengers around me woke up, but I hadn't slept for a second.

At that very moment, I was farther away from home than I had ever been. And yet I heard myself saying words that made complete sense to me:

"I'm home."

2

"The Ax Forgets;
the Tree Remembers"

She is tall and statuesque.
   Her smile is radiant.
   She radiates warmth, energy, excitement.

Those were my first thoughts when I saw Dr. Angelou walk off the plane. During our brief encounter in Los Angeles, she had been seated. I hadn't realized that her full height was more than six feet. Her physical presence was impressive. She wore a long multicolored cotton dress, a lively African print. She took long strides when she walked. Her gait was one of self-assurance and determination.

Julianne, Ruth, and I weren't the only ones at the

airport to greet her. There were reporters, photographers, and dozens of well-wishers, fans, and friends she had known during her four-year stay in West Africa. She graciously made her way through the crowd until she reached us. After embracing Julianne and Ruth, she looked directly into my eyes.

"And you must be young Tavis Smiley, the man about whom my dear friends speak so highly."

"I am," I said. "I can't tell you how much I appreciate this invitation, Dr. Angelou. It's a great honor."

"I'm glad you could make it, young Tavis. Is this your first time out of the country?"

"Other than a quick trip across the Detroit border to Windsor, Ontario, yes."

"Why, that's wonderful. If, from time to time, I seem to be looking through your eyes, that's only because I want to have as fresh a view as possible."

Ah, my heart sang. That was something I could help her do. That I wanted to do.

After she and the ladies exchanged a few words, we were ready to go. I took her bags and accompanied her to the waiting van.

Our hotel, the commodious Golden Tulip, was only five minutes from the airport. But before she had a chance to check in, a government official arrived to inform Dr.

Angelou that she was to be a guest at the residence of Ghana's president, Jerry John Rawlings.

"Give me a short while to settle in," she told us before being whisked away. "And then we'll all get together and catch up."

When the evening call came, Dr. Angelou invited Julianne, Ruth, and me to visit her at the presidential residence, a large but unpretentious compound. Her guest suite consisted of a bedroom and sitting room overlooking a garden. We were served a strong brew of tea in the garden.

I was still jet-lagged, my mind overstimulated, my spirit overexcited. Aside from the trip from the airport to the hotel and from the hotel to the residence, I had seen little of Accra. I had, of course, seen that everyone was black. That's the first thing any visitor to Africa notes. For an African American, that's an emotional revelation. That was especially true for me because I had grown up in the white world of rural Indiana. My high school, which sat next to a cornfield, was 98 percent white. Now I was in a black world, in a black country that was a small part of an enormous black continent.

These were my private thoughts as I listened to Julianne, Ruth, and Dr. Angelou exchange news about their private lives and careers. I listened attentively, but at the same time purposely sat back. I didn't want to appear too eager to enter the conversation—even though I was. It was enough to see the warm camaraderie among the women and the mutual respect they extended one another. These were three accomplished and fascinating women. Dr. Angelou was quick to ask questions of her friends and careful not to dominate the discussion.

As they spoke, I breathed in the fresh night air. The sky was aglow with a million stars. The garden was filled with large leafy plants whose exotic fragrance fueled my natural high.

"Young Tavis Smiley," said Dr. Angelou, breaking my reverie. "Something tells me that at this very moment, you must be entertaining all sorts of new feelings. It's strange and quite wonderful for Americans like us to step on African soil for the first time, isn't it?"

"You're reading my mind, Dr. Angelou," I said, surprised and grateful for the attention.

"Before this trip, how did you picture Africa?"

I had done reading, of course, but I had to admit that my main visual images came from the Tarzan movies I had seen as a child.

Dr. Angelou laughed heartily. "Mine were exactly the same! I, too, made it a point to study the cultural and political history. I thought because I had lived and worked in Cairo I had some intimacy with this continent. But Egypt has its own glorious and complex culture. The vast Africa that lives below the Sahara—black Africa, the Africa that birthed our forebears—that's the Africa about which I had scant understanding. I knew that Hollywood had trivialized and made a mockery of our heritage, but that didn't keep those images from floating across my imagination. Hollywood makes a mighty impression, especially on impressionable youth. That's one of the reasons I think it's so vital for young people to travel as soon as they are able. To challenge those manipulated images with raw reality is a life-changing experience. My hope is that this trip, young Tavis, might have such an effect on you."

I nodded. "My hope as well, Dr. Angelou."

"Speaking of Hollywood," she said, "I recently reread Jimmy's book *The Devil Finds Work*, a group of essays he wrote about cinema and published in the seventies. Do you know it?"

I had to think fast. I had an inkling who "Jimmy" was, but I wasn't sure.

"Are you talking about James Baldwin?" I had to ask.

"Yes."

I wanted to say that I did know other works by Baldwin, but what would be the point? "I don't know that book," I confessed.

"It's brilliant," she said. "But of course Jimmy was a brilliant man. I love his novels and plays and essays, but in this, a critique of how Hollywood treats the Negro, he's at his sharpest. His perceptions about the bias in American filmmaking are priceless."

For the next several minutes, she described in depth some of the political and literary links that tied her to Baldwin. Her affection for him was apparent.

"Wasn't James Baldwin one of the people who encouraged you to write your first memoir?" I asked, finding—at last—an appropriate way into the dialogue.

"It took Jimmy and an army of others to persuade me," said Dr. Angelou. "But that's another topic for another day."

I wanted to know more about that topic. In fact, I wanted to know everything about Dr. Angelou. I wanted to keep the conversation going for hours and was disappointed when the evening ended on the early side. For all I knew, this might be my last extended visit with her. Naturally I'd go to her lecture at the W. E. B. Du Bois Centre, but between now and then she might well have appointments and excursions that excluded me.

Sensing my eagerness and insecurity, she reassured me. "Look here, young Tavis Smiley, while we're in Accra we'll have lots of time to solve the world's problems together. I promise you that we'll talk until the cows come home. Tomorrow we will venture into the city, where you'll meet new people and see new things. So get ready."

At that point she broke into song. It was an old hymn that I knew from the Pentecostal church in which I was raised.

I want to be ready
I want to be ready
I want to be ready
To walk in Jerusalem

John said the city was just four-square
Walk in Jerusalem just like John
And he declared he'd meet me there
Walk in Jerusalem just like John

Because I knew the song well, I couldn't help but sing along.

When Peter was preaching at Pentecost
Walk in Jerusalem just like John
He was endowed with the Holy Ghost
Walk in Jerusalem just like John

If you get there before I do
Walk in Jerusalem just like John
Tell all my friends I'm a-coming too
Walk in Jerusalem just like John

Dr. Angelou's singing voice was filled with joy. If I had been intimidated by being in the company of a world-class intellectual, the intimidation melted the moment she broke into song. Suddenly we had a common text between us, a sacred text: shared childhood memories of the comfort afforded by a church in which the God of love was worshipped and praised.

Before going to sleep, I thanked God for this trip and for the privilege of being in Dr. Angelou's company. Never had I met a person so fully engaged, so ready to listen, so ready to share, so eager to embrace the moment with a full heart. Even after grueling hours of international jet travel, her enthusiasm was fresh. She was as excited as I was to be in Africa.

Too keyed up to sleep, I picked up *All God's Children Need Traveling Shoes* and reread the passages where Dr. Angelou described the "broad avenues" and "unpaved rutted lanes" of Accra and how they "became gorgeous with moving pageantry." She drew a landscape of hand-carts and bicycles, the market women "balancing large baskets on their heads as they proudly swung their wide hips," the musical sounds of the Twi language, the "too sweet" aromas of the flowers and fried fish, the honking of horns and the beating of drums, "the muddle of many languages shouted or murmured," the glorious cacophony of the capital city.

The next morning, her words came alive as I saw for myself the picture she had painted perfectly. I saw the glorious city, in all its scrambled complexity, as a page from her book. I kept seeing people who looked like my uncle or my aunt, my father, my mother, my sisters and brothers, my cousins and my friends. In their features—in the piercing expression in someone's eyes or the distinctive shape of someone's body—I recognized a striking similarity to black people I knew. A million miles away from home, I was indeed at home.

John and Mary Ellen Ray, Dr. Angelou's and Ruth Love's dear friends in Ghana, made me feel even more at home. Their small house was modest, but their loving hospitality enormous. John Ray—who was always called by his full name—was a photographer, and he and Mary Ellen had expatriated to Ghana back in the 1960s, several years before Dr. Angelou first visited. They had stayed in touch ever since.

"These are the folks who saw me through," said Dr. Angelou after making the introductions. "I was actually just passing through Accra on my way to Nigeria when I met these wonderful people. They said, 'Maya, you must stay. You have arrived in the sweetest spot in all of Africa. We promise you—you'll do no better.' But I wouldn't listen. Besides, I had work waiting for me in Nigeria. I just couldn't imagine staying in Ghana. I was still operating on the arrogant principle, so common among the young, that the world would bend to my will. Had she been around, my grandmother would quickly inform me that our job is do the Lord's will. But among hardheaded writers and artists such as myself, willfulness, my dears, is an occupational hazard. My felicitous stay in Accra helped me overcome that hazard. I saw that God was doing for me what I, in my single-mindedness, could not have done for myself. Left to my own devices, I would have missed out completely on my miraculous Ghanaian experience."

"Your son was in that terrible car accident, Maya," said Mary Ellen. "That's what kept you here, wasn't it?"

"Yes, of course. When the news reached me, I was beside myself. All I was told was that his condition was critical. This is my only child, mind you. My life, my heart. Guy was about to start college. His adult life was just beginning. Thank God he survived. But his extended hospitalization meant that I'd have to forgo my job in Nigeria and stay in Ghana. That's how the blessing arrived—through near tragedy. From then on, I've tried to remind myself that even the harshest news may well carry a blessing. It might take a day, a week, a year, or even a lifetime for that blessing to manifest, but manifest it will. Young Tavis Smiley here will remind us what the pious church ladies have to say about God's perfect timing."

Without missing a beat, I said, "The Lord may not be there when you call Him, but He's always right on time."

"Let the church say, 'Amen,'" said Dr. Angelou.

This exchange made me so happy that I couldn't wipe the smile off my face.

As Dr. Angelou and her friends exchanged news about recent events in their lives, both big and small, I saw how, even in a home that was not her own, Dr. Angelou acted as host. It wasn't anything overt. It wasn't as though she took over conversations or the planning of activities. You could never accuse her of ruling the roost. She was far too attuned to our emotional needs to step on our toes. It was her energy, her spirit, her unbridled joy in telling stories—and eliciting stories from us—that made her the focal point. If she was the earth, we were stars in her orbit. She did more than make us feel welcome; she made us luminous.

But she did that for all the people in her circle—made them know they were appreciated. That afternoon we went to a middle school where a teacher had prepared a student dance program in Dr. Angelou's honor. In their boldly colorful garb, the girls moved with not only extraordinary dexterity but also grace. Their accompaniment was drumming provided by their male classmates, who, I later learned, were forging polyrhythms on the djembe, the skin-covered, bongolike instrument employed by West Africa's master drummers. These kids already sounded like masters to me.

When the program was over, Dr. Angelou, with tears in her eyes, hugged and kissed each performer—girls and boys alike—and, in their native tongue, addressed them at length.

The kids were surprised. They were eager to show off the English they had learned for this occasion. Understanding what was required, Dr. Angelou switched to her own native tongue.

"I'd love to hear you speak my language," she said. "But before that let me simply thank you for your dazzling display of talent."

One by one, the children identified themselves and delivered their individual versions of a common message:

"Dr. Maya Angelou, we welcome you back. We love you as though you were our mother. Please return to Ghana soon."

After the performance we drove to a café that was a favorite of Mary Ellen and John Ray's.

"I remember it well," said Dr. Angelou. "They serve the best spicy rice in all of Ghana."

I had my first taste of kelewele, plantains fried in palm oil with crushed ginger. It was delicious and crunchy.

Dr. Angelou was still marveling at the dance performance.

She began speaking about Pearl Primus, the legendary dancer who had been her instructor in New York.

"She was a brilliant woman, a learned anthropologist as well as a top-notch choreographer. She championed African dance. She lectured extensively on the beautiful complexity of African culture. Mind you, this was back in the forties, when those Tarzan movies were at their height. It was Miss Primus who turned Langston Hughes's lovely poem 'The Negro Speaks of Rivers' into a dance. She went south to study the music and dances of our people in Mississippi and Georgia, going from the country churches to the cotton fields. She went to Africa, where she researched dance in Senegal, then the Belgian Congo, Angola, and Liberia. In Nigeria she learned their dance so completely that they called her Omowale, the child who had come back to her native home.

"When I met Pearl Primus, in the fifties, I was naturally intimidated but mightily motivated. I was determined to learn everything this marvelous woman had to teach. I attended every one of her lecture-demonstrations on African dance. I joined her class for four separate sessions over the course of a year. Believe me, she was a taskmaster who suffered no fools. She had not the least tolerance for mediocrity. I practiced night and day, adhering to her rigorous methodology. When it was over, she said that I had a decent chance of becoming a decent dancer. Beyond that, she saw in me the ability to become a teacher myself. Coming from her, that was high praise.

"I took the spirit of Pearl Primus and did indeed become a teacher of dance. I found work in Cleveland at a cultural center headed by educated Negroes. My intention was to do for the children what Pearl Primus had done for me: instruct them in the wonders of African dance. The students were young and eager and full of energy. I adored them. They adored my lessons. I had no problems with my girls. It was the mothers who came down on me."

"For what reason?" I asked.

"The mothers, many of whom had degrees from colleges like Spelman and Bennett and Barnard, asked, 'Why are you teaching them African dances?'

"'Because they are quite beautiful,' I answered, 'and beautifully expressive.'

"'We prefer modern dance.'

"'Sorry, dear ladies, I do not teach so-called modern dance. I have a mandate to teach the dances of our ancestors. It is a part of our illustrious heritage that we need to reclaim.'

"'We didn't lose anything in Africa. We are in America. We are modern Americans, and our daughters want to learn modern dance.'

"'Your daughters are loving what they've learned so

far,' I said, but my words fell on deaf ears. My teaching days at that bourgeois cultural center were numbered. I was out of there in no time. But the experience impressed me deeply. I thought long and hard about how our African history had been clothed in garments of guilt and toxic shame. Think about the slaves who were ripped from their kin. Forced to learn a completely foreign tongue, they suffered one of the greatest losses any people can suffer: the inability to tell stories. When we lose the griot, the master African storyteller, we lose ourselves—our history, our connection to the mysteries of life. We lose ourselves.

"To my mind, my students' socially ambitious mothers had lost that precious link and, even worse, were glad because of it. They looked at Africa as nothing more than a land of savages. They thus sought to disassociate themselves from such savagery. It was painful for me to realize that these women, like the ancestors they were unwilling to claim, had, sadly, adopted the attitude of our slave owners, who saw us as beasts of burden. The old African proverb says, 'The ax forgets; the tree remembers.' I saw how horrifically it injured us to identify with our oppressors. If we were to keep our souls whole, we couldn't afford to forget. We had to remember.

"Pearl Primus had taught me that to reclaim Africa was to reclaim not only our essential humanity but also our unique genius as storytellers. After Guy's accident, after he enrolled in college in Accra, and after I was able to settle down and find the right rhythm and rhymes to my life here, I experienced the truth of Pearl Primus's lessons. I experienced Africa as though it were my mother. I experienced Africa as my teacher. Because Africa put me back in touch with my righteous roots, I began to grapple with the stories of my own past and re-alize that eventually these stories would have to be told."

"You saw yourself as a griot," I said.

"That's a lovely way of putting it, young Tavis Smiley. Now I can embrace such nomenclature. Back then, though, when I was in my thirties and still in the midst of my African journey, I would not have claimed such a noble title. I still had a long way to go."

"But Africa was a critical point." I saw it had been for her.

"Indeed," said Dr. Angelou. "As I trust it will be a critical turning point for you."

3

"Frailties and Faults"

Wherever we traveled in Ghana, Dr. Angelou attracted crowds. Even people who didn't know her sensed that she was someone special. The fact that she was dispensing love with such natural and joyful ease drew people to her.

She greeted well-wishers with patience and reciprocated by displaying an interest in those interested in her. She also shunned adulation. If someone was too effusive with flattery, she could be somewhat stern.

On the afternoon that we went to the university so she could greet a few old colleagues, she agreed to meet a group of students. During the colloquy, one young woman, overwhelmed by being in Dr. Angelou's presence, spoke of her as a kind of literary goddess.

"Please, child," said Dr. Angelou. "I am many things, but a deity I am not. We all contain elements of the divine, but I can tell you that I am definitely of this earth. If you see me as saintly, you are not seeing me at all."

Seeing that the student was taken aback, Dr. Angelou added, "I don't want to sound harsh, my dear, but I grow alarmed when I see young people absorbed in the cult of personality. All that does is distance you from the person you admire. If I drink in your worshipful praise and allow it to inflate my ego, I am injured. If you continue such praise and elevate me to a place where I am no longer a flawed human, your sense of self is diminished, and you are injured."

After the symposium, when the students had all left and I had a few minutes alone with Dr. Angelou, I spoke about my adulation of Dr. Martin Luther King Jr.

"I have a hard time thinking of him as anything but superhuman," I explained.

Before she responded to my statement, she asked when I had first become familiar with Dr. King.

"You had to have been very young," she said.

"I was. I was only three when he was assassinated and had no real memory of that. But when I was twelve I was in the first real crisis of my life."

"What happened?" asked Dr. Angelou.

I was reluctant to get personal. The incident was something I had hardly talked about. But I was flattered and, quite frankly, excited by the interest that Dr. Angelou showed in me. Having read her memoirs, I knew something of the excruciating emotional crises she had faced as a young girl. Compared with hers, mine seemed trivial. When I told her that, she was quick to respond.

"Since time immemorial wise people have been saying that all comparisons are odious. When we compare, we set up a winner-loser dynamic. If my crisis is greater than yours, then yours is belittled and insignificant. I say that's nonsense. Each crisis has its own power, its own unique reality. What was the reality of yours, Tavis?"

With a heady mixture of reluctance and eagerness, I told the story of how our church's minister had falsely accused my sister and me of misbehaving in Sunday School. The accusation was leveled at us during a service when my parents were present. The public humiliation sent my dad into a rage. That evening he beat us so severely we had to be hospitalized for weeks. As a result, social services took us from our parents. My sister never went back home. Ultimately I did, but it took years for my heart to heal.

When I was still in the hospital, wondering why in the world I had been subjected to such cruel punishment, a member of our church brought me a box of old LP records on the Motown label. These were the speeches of Martin Luther King Jr. Those speeches changed my world. They gave me a sense of purpose. They gave me hope. They sparked my energy and had me believing in the force of redemptive love.

Given all that, how in the world could I ever think of Martin Luther King Jr. as a mere mortal?

"Oh, I see," said Dr. Angelou. She said those three words—"Oh, I see"—as though my own words had touched her soul. I could see that she felt the pain I had felt. I knew then that she had not merely been listening to me with her ears but also with her heart.

"Your story is a precious one, Tavis, and it must sit in the center of who you were, who you are now, and who you will be. I love your story because it is a transformative tale. That event—that unprovoked beating— might well have been one of those upside-down blessings whose manifestation is not known until decades later. To be energized in a positive way is always a blessing, regardless of the source.

"I can well understand why it is difficult for you to see Dr. King as a mere man. But I can assure you that he was. Like Malcolm X or Medgar Evers or Fannie Lou Hamer, Martin was an ordinary human being who lived in extraordinary times and was able to do extraordinary things. It's the ordinariness of these people that allows us to connect to them. We can relax in our ordinariness and enjoy the humility that ordinariness brings. Only then can we really feel their presence. Rather than be intimidated, we are able to draw closer to them. In that way, Dr. King is not a distant figure sitting on a distant throne. Instead he is an intimate, a father, a friend, a brother."

"You must have been devastated by his death," I said.

I knew it but hadn't put two and two together.

"April fourth, as you may well know, is my birthday.

"More specifically, April fourth, 1968, was my fortieth birthday. It was a day when I had been invited to join him in Memphis to support the garbage workers. I was already committed to the Poor People's Campaign, which he envisioned as an even greater event than the 1963 March on Washington. I was quite active in the New York branch of the Southern Christian Leadership Conference. Martin and I had become close. I had every intention of devoting a full month to helping him raise money to bring the Poor People's Campaign to Washington, DC. His vision was to erect a tent city where all the poor—black, white, brown, yellow, and red—would claim ground and not move until Congress took action. But my participation would have to wait until after my birthday. You see, I was giving a party for my hip and sophisticated New York friends from the Harlem Writers Guild. I was cooking a six-course dinner for twenty. I was going all out. I was in the middle of my preparations when my sister friend came running into the kitchen. 'Maya! Maya! It can't be true!' 'What are you talking about, child?' Then those words were spoken. Martin was gone. I was gone. The world, the country, the hope for our future seemed gone. I was devastated. All I knew was that I couldn't be alone in my apartment on Ninety-Seventh Street. I'd have to go out and walk up to Harlem. Yes, I had to be on the streets of Harlem. It was there where strangers stopped me to say, 'Why?' and my reply was the same: 'Why?' *Why? Why? Why?* It's the only word that made sense. Just to hear that one word again and again—covered in tears, spoken in unspeakable pain—got me through the nightmare.

"For years, out of respect, I stopped celebrating my birthday. To do so seemed obscene. But then one year I received a lovely bouquet of flowers from Coretta Scott King. Someone had told her that my birthday fell upon the day she had lost her husband, and, out of the kindness of her heart, she took the time to wish me well. With Coretta's blessing, I took to celebrating my birthday again. On April fourth, it became a yearly ritual that Coretta and I would send each other flowers, as if their sweet fragrance might take the terrible sting out of the memory, at least for a moment. Though to be honest,

Tavis, my birthday became one of heartbreaking conflict—joy for having been born and given the privilege of this human journey and grief for the loss of my dear friend."

To be seated next to a close friend of Dr. King's—and to have her speak at length and with love about his legacy—was a rare privilege. I couldn't help but ask her more questions about the man I considered the greatest democratic public intellectual America has ever produced.

In her response, Dr. Angelou seemed worried about what she considered my idolatrous attitude.

"You want me to tell you stories about his greatness, Tavis, when I feel the need to tell you stories about his salty humor. The man loved to laugh. He was famous for practical jokes. He loved the same church hymns that you and I love, but he also loved the funky soul music of James Brown. Yes, he listened to Mahalia, but he also listened to Sam and Dave. He was an earthy man, a grounded man, a man who might be talking with sanitation workers one day and with the king of Sweden the next. Because he was comfortable in his own skin, he was comfortable everywhere."

I was about to reply but didn't. Sensing my hesitancy, Dr. Angelou said, "You are still not satisfied with my response, are you, Tavis?"

I wasn't. For all that was normal about Dr. King, I knew there had been extraordinary moments of achievement in his life that Dr. Angelou had witnessed. I wanted to hear about those moments. I wanted to hear, over and over again, how great this man really was. I was not interested in learning about his shortcomings. At the same time, as a child growing up in a strict religious household, I had been taught never to challenge adults. Such behavior was strictly forbidden.

Now, on a university campus in Accra, Ghana, in a dialogue with Dr. Maya Angelou, those lessons came back to me. And amazingly, Dr. Angelou understood just what was holding me back.

"Speak your mind, young Tavis Smiley," she said. "Just as Dr. King never objected to intelligent opposition, neither do I. I welcome it. If you start treating me with the same saintly respect as the student I just met, we're going to have a hard time of it—I guarantee you. You're an educated man. You're a curious man. You have a brain. You have a point of view. Let's have it!"

I was startled by Dr. Angelou's invitation. I say that because my childhood conditioning, which forbade arguing with elders, had, until that moment, held me in check. I didn't realize how strongly that conditioning had restrained me until Maya shattered the restraint.

I took up her challenge because her challenge was

couched in concern for my intellectual integrity. I could feel that she wanted to help me. And because when Dr. Angelou talks to you, and you feel like you have every last bit of her attention and compassion, you must respond. Thus I gathered up my courage and spoke.

"There are two elements here," I said. "There are Dr. King's singular achievements. We have to agree that those were remarkable. When I think of the remarkable social changes he effected in the wake of tremendous adversity, I'm awestruck. That is his public side. His private side is another matter. I can revere his accomplishments as a public man and ignore his faults as a private man."

"Then you'll be ignoring the essential humanity that sits at the heart of who Martin was. Don't you understand, Tavis, that his frailties and faults put his accomplishments in a brighter light? They let us know that frailties and faults accompany even the most accomplished among us. They are a critical part not only of the whole human package but also of the blessed mess that makes us people—short of God's perfection, yet always desirous of God's perfect love."

"Scripture says, 'A perfect love casts out all fear.'"

"Yes, dear Tavis, but it does not say that all of us— or, for that matter, any of us—will achieve that perfect love. It points to the fact that the pursuit of such love will diminish our fears and thus enrich our lives. We are in pursuit of such love. You are. I am. And certainly Martin was. Yet it is not the perfection of his character that inspires me but rather the imperfection."

"We're all cracked vessels."

"Precisely—even those we want to idolize," she said.

"I suppose you'd say that I'm hiding from the truth," I told her. Because of her I was beginning to see that maybe I was.

Rather than respond with spoken words, Dr. Angelou broke into another song from her grandmother's church:

There's no hiding place down here
You know, there's no hiding place down here
I went to the rock to hide my face
But the rock cried out no hiding place
There's no hiding place down here…

4

"I Do Not Care to Dance"

Dr. Angelou's company—spending whole *days* in it—
overloaded my emotional circuitry. Thus far our time
alone had been limited, but she had been gracious
enough to include me in all her excursions, from formal
meetings with government officials to intimate encounters with Julianne, Ruth, and her friends Mary Ellen and
John Ray. In all situations she generated excitement. People were excited by her presence. And she was just as
excited by them.

What was the source of the excitement that Dr. Angelou generated?

It was how she demonstrated—in both word and

deed—the pleasures derived from merely being alive. As a speaker and listener, she expressed inextinguishable enthusiasm. The world she inhabited was filled with wonder. And because she was always welcoming you into her world, you felt privileged to be in her company.

One day, for instance, she wanted to go into the bush.

"You'll want to see some of the wildlife that inhabits this gorgeous country," she told us. "The beauty of the plants and birds is something to behold."

A government car was put at Dr. Angelou's disposal. Seated in back, I watched her close her eyes and breathe in the morning air.

"Glorious," she said after opening her eyes. "Simply glorious."

Fearlessly, she traipsed around the countryside with the spirit of a young city child viewing nature for the first time.

"Maya is sixty-four going on six," said Mary Ellen.

"Oh, thank you, dear sister," said Dr. Angelou. "That's the sweetest thing you could possibly say about me."

"It's her joie de vivre," Ruth explained later that same day. "The moment she opens her eyes each morning, she's off and running. She once told me that her morning mantra is, 'Ah, the creative possibilities this day will surely bring.' She exudes optimism."

Even without the living example of Dr. Angelou to inspire me, Africa stimulated my senses, too, especially at night, when, with my window open and the breezes flowing through, I heard the calls and cries of distant creatures, a music all its own. The scents were potent and pleasing, filling me with a longing for more knowledge, more life experience. I went to the window and looked up. The moon was full and shaded in pale yellow.

I couldn't sleep. I looked over the pile of books I had brought with me, most of which I had already consumed—histories of Ghana; W. E. B. Du Bois's classic *The Souls of Black Folk;* several of Dr. Angelou's memoirs. I picked up my well-marked copy of *All God's Children Need Traveling Shoes* and went to the passages where she discussed her meetings with Malcolm X in Ghana. If the opportunity arose, I'd ask her about those meetings. I'd question her about everything. With a thousand questions still running through my head, I struggled to turn off the motor inside my mind. Finally— and gratefully—I succumbed to sleep, not long before day broke around me. Yet in my dreams I was still thinking up questions, still preoccupied with learning all I could and making the most of this adventure.

"You are a highly motivated young man," said Dr. Angelou the next day when we were back at the presidential palace enjoying a casual lunch. Without saying a word, I knew that she saw all the questions lined up in my mind.

"I applaud motivation," she said. "Motivation is a precious commodity. I've often said that of all the virtues courage is the most vital. Without courage we can do little. Even love requires courage. But motivation is, in part, a form of courage—especially when our motivation allows us to get to extraordinary places and do extraordinary things."

"Accra is certainly an extraordinary place," I said.

"I'm not sure John Ray and Mary Ellen see it as such," said Dr. Angelou, looking over at her friends. "Am I right?"

Mary Ellen replied that, while she had fallen in love with the Ghanaians and their lovely country decades earlier, it was the *absence* of the extraordinary that brought her and John Ray to Africa. She explained that it was the low-key and ordinary way of life that had attracted them.

"*Ordinary* is a beautiful word," said Dr. Angelou, "because it implies simplicity. The expatriates I knew during my time here, like my sister Mary Ellen and brother John Ray, were seeking, as was I, an alternative to America, where the racial question was indeed extraordinary—so much so that it never left one's consciousness. To live in a black nation where blackness is as ordinary as the blueness of the sky or the greenness of the ocean—ah, what a comfort that can be! What a relief! I think that's one of the things that the expatriate seeks—relief from a culture riddled with conflict."

"But surely there was critical conflict in Ghana," I pushed back. "President Kwame Nkrumah, whom you admired so much, was toppled by a military coup in the sixties, just after you returned home to the United States."

"I am pleased that you know your history," said Dr. Angelou—she often interspersed such formal phrasings in her conversation—"and of course there isn't a country or culture in this whole wide world that does not embody deep conflicts, whether political or religious or psychological. But the expatriate is blessed with a certain naïveté that provides a cushion from these conflicts. The expatriate doesn't always see beneath the surface of his or her new setting. This is a new setting for you, Tavis, and while I'm certain you have studied this continent and country until your eyes turned red, the newness is, above all, what you see, feel, hear, taste, and touch. And there's nothing wrong with that. Newness has its own sweet rewards. The first time, for instance, that we hear Charlie Parker's saxophone we may not know of the complexities in his life that contributed to his unique sound. But that's okay. The first-time experience has a joy all its own—the first time watching Judith Jamison dance, the first viewing of a Jacob Lawrence cityscape, the first sip of Champagne, the first taste of foie gras."

"What about the first time you met Malcolm X?" I asked. "He must have made a mighty big impression."

Dr. Angelou smiled. "I'm guessing that query is high on your list of questions to ask," she said good-naturedly.

"It is," I said with undisguised eagerness. "Given how diligently you worked for Dr. King, I'd love to hear how you walked the line between him and Malcolm X."

"Effortlessly," Dr. Angelou was quick to respond. "It was a straight line between two men driven by a passion to help their people."

"Yet with two dramatically different pathways to achieve that end."

"All this must be put in context," she said. "It was 1961. I was living in New York, where I was active in the Cultural Association for Women of African Heritage. Our purpose was to support all civil rights activities. For the most part we were artists and teachers. I had just learned that Patrice Lumumba, the first democrati-cally elected prime minister of the independent Congo, the former Belgian colony, had been murdered. Rumors were circulating that the CIA was involved. You must remember that in the early sixties, when the hope of pan-

Africanism was still very much alive, we looked to Lumumba, Sékou Touré of Guinea, and Kwame Nkrumah as a holy trinity of leaders with substantial intellectual and moral weight. Lumumba's death was devastating.

"While still carrying the shocking news inside my head, I was coming out of the National Memorial African Bookstore on Seventh Avenue in the heart of Harlem. Lewis Michaux, the store owner, was a mentor to many of us aspiring writers. To me, his place was heaven on earth. It was teeming with tomes unavailable anywhere else. The walls were covered with photographs and posters of black leaders and artists. For people like Ralph Ellison and Jimmy Baldwin, this remarkable bookstore was sacred ground. I went for comfort, stimulation, and information.

"The minute I left the store, I saw that a large crowd had gathered across the street. It was a rally organized by the Nation of Islam. Standing on a platform was Malcolm X. This was the first time I saw him in the flesh. No matter what my prior thoughts about the Nation might have been, I was held tight in his rhetorical grip. He was forceful. He was persuasive. He was eloquent. His anger at the white world that had subjugated our people corresponded with my own anger. There are times, Tavis, when anger, suppressed over centuries, requires expression. This was such a time. I saw his words as knives cutting into the corrupt heart of the dominant culture. I had to applaud those words. I had to give thanks to God that a man like this appeared at the time that he did. If my name for God was different from Malcolm's, that didn't matter in the least. All that mattered was that he appeared on the streets of Harlem that afternoon as a spokesman for pride. No one could deny the deep compassion he expressed for black people. Some saw him as an instrument of hate. I saw him as an instrument of love.

"That very night I decided to organize a protest that we would take into the General Assembly of the United Nations when Ambassador Adlai Stevenson was set to announce the sad news of Lumumba's passing. It was Lewis Michaux who helped us spread the word. I always said that, when it came to disseminating news in Harlem, Mr. Michaux was the man. His blessed bookstore was a hotbed of political action. Yes, sir, there was high drama surrounding the protest. We marched on the streets outside the UN and, once inside, were thrown out of the assembly. We made the evening news. I considered our operation successful. In the aftermath, I saw the need for more such operations. And, if you can believe my gall, Tavis, I took it upon myself to solicit the support of Malcolm X himself. I called the Nation and asked for a private appointment. My friends were surprised when I told them that the minister would see me.

"Next thing I knew I was walking into the Muslim restaurant in Harlem. I announced myself, saying that I was there to see Brother Malcolm. Within seconds he appeared. He was cordial and quite direct. He looked straight into my eyes. I began to speak of our protest at the UN; I said we expected fifty people and wound up with over a thousand in our ranks.

" 'I am aware of that protest,' he said. 'But how does that involve the Nation?'

" 'We are desirous of the Nation's support in future protests,' I said.

"Malcolm went on to explain that the Nation did not involve itself in protest. He explained that such demonstrations simply buy into the political paradigm that he summarily rejected. He further said that I was misdirecting the anger of black people by channeling that energy into marches and sit-ins. Respectfully, I challenged his view. The murder of Lumumba, I said, demanded protest. How could we merely stand idly by and do nothing? He answered that, despite the good I believed our demonstrations were doing, conservative blacks would rise up against us. They would accuse us of disturbing the status quo. He predicted that they would see us as too radical. They would argue that we were misrepresenting the majority of black people. As you might guess, Malcolm's predictions proved true."

"And yet you did not become a Muslim," I pointed out. "You joined forces with Dr. King."

"Though in doing so, I did not lose any respect for Malcolm. His insights into the systemic and pathological racism of this country were powerful. He understood the reactionary nature of the black middle class. I'd remind you that Martin himself was seen as far too radical by the vast majority of the black religious leaders of his time. They didn't like the idea of getting their hands dirty by holding placards and marching on the streets. Respectable Negroes did not comport themselves in such a fashion."

"But then again," said Dr. Angelou's friend Mary Ellen, "when Malcolm came to Ghana, he was an entirely different man from the Malcolm you met in Harlem. Isn't that true, Maya?"

"Very true. Malcolm arrived some time after Martin's famous March on Washington."

"We had a march of our own, right here in Accra," said Mary Ellen.

"Indeed we did, my dear sister! Julian Mayfield, you, John Ray, and the rest of our so-called radical crowd decided to show our solidarity by marching in front of the American embassy in Accra at the same time the March on Washington was being held. That meant midnight Africa time. I might remind you that my support for

Dr. King had gone through several major changes. After working for him and seeing the violent reaction to his nonviolence, I myself gave up on nonviolence. I thought he was fooling himself by thinking that pure Christian love would turn the tide in his favor. I was not about to turn the other cheek. This was another reason why, before I left the country for Africa, Malcolm was making increasingly more sense to me. At the same time, I felt obligated to back any major demonstration supporting civil rights. And from what we read in the international press, the 1963 march was shaping up as a major event."

"And you remember what happened that night, don't you, Maya?" asked Mary Ellen, gently moving Maya along.

"Of course. Julian was late in arriving at our protest. We were all looking for him. When he finally arrived, he was carrying news that none of us wanted to hear. Dr. Du Bois was dead. He had been ill for some time. He had lived until the age of ninety-five, and all of us marveled that his passing coincided with the high drama of the March on Washington. When word came to Washington, Roy Wilkins of the NAACP delivered the sad news to the great assembly and asked for a moment of silence."

"Is that something you'll talk about when you deliver your lecture later this week?" I asked Dr. Angelou.

"I'll probably touch upon it, Tavis, because the timing was so incredible."

"And then, as if there weren't enough excitement, we learned that Malcolm was coming to Accra," said Mary Ellen.

"That happened the following summer. And as you said, he was a far different Malcolm from the man I met that day in Harlem. He had been to Mecca and was changed entirely. His first night in Accra he met all us expatriates in Julian's home. His sharp edges had softened. I remember he said that when he returned home he would make statements that would surely shock everyone. He had been reexamining many of his earlier convictions. He said that in Mecca he had met white men with blue eyes whom he could call brother. He had a new vision of the brotherhood of man that went beyond race. He saw the essential humanity of all people. And he had broken ties with the Nation of Islam.

"I was both surprised and pleased. Because my own political outlook had changed so much during these tumultuous years, I was glad to see that a man as brilliant as Malcolm could also change and, in critical ways, repudiate his earlier philosophy. He said he had come to the Motherland to rally the African leaders in support of American blacks. He planned to present that cause before the United Nations, and, rather than depend upon the goodwill of what Martin had labeled 'fair-minded' white Americans, he and his African brothers would stand as one before the world court. He said, 'If South African blacks can petition the UN against their country's policy of apartheid, then America should be shown on the world's stage as a repressionist and bestial racist nation.' We applauded wildly.

"He was with us in Ghana for a week—and what a week it was! He lectured at the university, where I was teaching in the music and drama department. The title of his incendiary speech was 'Will Africa Ignite America's Racial Powder Keg?' And of course he spoke brilliantly. I remember thinking how seamlessly he merged the rhetoric of the black preacher with the logic of the academic intellectual. He addressed the Ghanaian parliament, and, after much effort on our part, we were able to get him a meeting with President Nkrumah. Malcolm described that meeting as the highest honor he had yet received in Africa."

"Remember the big party that the Ghana Press Club gave him?" asked Mary Ellen.

"Indeed I do!" Dr. Angelou replied. "Every journalist in the country came to greet him. There was music and dancing. I recall watching him as a troupe danced the highlife, a sensual dance that was enormously popular in West Africa. He smiled broadly but restrained himself.

I'll never forget his remarks. He thanked the press club for the gathering, but then he said, 'I do not care to dance. I think of our brothers and sisters at home, squirming under the heel of racial oppression, and I do not care to dance. I think of our brothers and sisters in the Congo, squirming under the heel of imperialist invasion, and I do not care to dance.' What a powerful statement!"

"And then there was that final encounter," said John Ray. "It happened on the morning when he asked all of us to join the entourage that drove him to the airport. That was the morning he ran into Muhammad Ali."

"We were shocked," said Dr. Angelou. "We didn't know Ali was in Ghana."

"The champ was checking into the hotel just as Malcolm was checking out," said John Ray.

"What a scene!" said Dr. Angelou. "The shock on their faces when they saw one another. It was so unexpected. Ali looked away, but Malcolm pursued him. He called after him. 'Brother Muhammad! Brother Muhammad!' When they came face-to-face, Malcolm spoke. I'll never forget his words. 'Brother, I still love you. You're still the greatest.' I could see that Ali wanted to return the love but could only speak of his disappointment that Malcolm had left the Honorable Elijah Muhammad. Malcolm did not try to explain himself. He knew that words would not matter. It was a poignant scene. Two brothers who had been close in America—now estranged in Africa. Later Julian Mayfield asked Malcolm if the encounter had surprised him. Malcolm replied that he understood the way Ali looked at the Honorable Elijah Muhammad as a father and a prophet. He said that, no matter what, Ali would always hold a special place in his heart.

"Julian also expressed concern that Malcolm, knowing that there was a price on his head, was traveling alone. There was no security. 'No one can guard anyone's life,' Malcolm said. 'Not even his own. Only Allah can protect. And he has let me slide so far.'"

"Before Malcolm left Ghana," I asked, "did you have a chance to have any private time with him?"

"I did," Dr. Angelou replied. "There were several evenings at Julian Mayfield's home when Malcolm and I spoke alone. He talked of forming a new group back home, the Organization of Afro-American Unity. Would I help? I said yes. I wasn't sure when I'd be coming home, but I wanted to be part of his movement. He said he would write me, and he did. Whenever a friend of his was coming to Ghana, he let me know so I might show him around. That included James Farmer, the head of CORE, the Congress of Racial Equality. In one of my letters to Malcolm I spoke of the need for leaders to speak to the people in language they can understand. He wrote me back and said he agreed. 'You can communicate,' he wrote, 'because you have plenty of soul and you always keep your feet firmly rooted on the ground.' Then he said, 'You are a beautiful writer and a beautiful woman.' He promised to help me in any way he could. I have to say that reading those words meant the world to me. I had written some journalism, but I had yet to publish a book. His encouragement touched me on the most profound level."

"And when you came back to the United States," I asked, "did you have a chance to meet with him again?"

"I came home in large part because of my determination to work with him. I knew that, given his renewed and remarkable humanity, he was on the verge of doing important things. I came back to the States and was at my mother's house in San Francisco. On the second day after my arrival my dear friend Ivonne called me. I hadn't seen her in years, so I was surprised when she said, 'Maya, girl, why in the world did you come back? These Negroes here are crazy. Did you hear how they killed that man in New York?'

"I didn't have to ask her who the man was. I knew. It was Malcolm X, gunned down at the Audubon Ballroom. It was February twenty-first, 1965."

For a long while we stayed silent.

"It was a blessing that you got to spend time with him here in Ghana," said Mary Ellen.

"A beautiful blessing," Dr. Angelou agreed. "But then again," she said, looking around at us, "being able to share our thoughts with another human being is a blessing."

5

Living History

One of my main memories of Africa involves school-rooms. Throughout our trip to Ghana, Dr. Angelou was always going to schools to interact with students—elementary schools, high schools, and colleges. She reveled in the pureness of the students' curiosity while they reveled in the sparkling enthusiasm of her very presence. The give-and-take was a beautiful thing to behold.

Most of those encounters were marked by easy exchanges. A student would ask how Maya became a writer. Another would ask about her days as a dancer and actress. Maya told each story as if she were telling it for the first time. She presented her past with a right-here, right-now relevance that never failed to fascinate. Once in a great while, though, she encountered a student with an attitude. I clearly remember one young man, a Ghanaian who had been schooled in England and had returned to Accra to complete a graduate degree. He rose to speak during the question-and-answer session after Dr. Angelou had delivered some brief remarks about the vitality of the black arts in present-day America—and how that vitality was fed by its rich African heritage. This took place in a university auditorium where every seat was filled.

Rather than ask a question, the young man delivered something of a monologue in which he pointed to the tradition of what he called self-mockery in African American entertainers. He said that the archetypes first developed in the early years of the twentieth century—the obsequious comics, the shuffling dancers, the bawdy blues mamas—were filled with a self-hatred that, according to his argument, characterized the American blacks even to this day. He cited any number of examples. He spoke with a self-assurance bordering on arrogance.

As he went on, I waited for Dr. Angelou to cut him off—but she didn't. She let him speak as long as he liked. I could see that others, like me, were uncomfortable with his diatribe. In a none-too-subtle way, he was accusing Dr. Angelou of having inherited the tradition of the Uncle Toms and the Aunt Jemimas, toothless characters all too willing to placate their oppressors.

When he was finally through, I breathed a sigh of relief. Knowing Dr. Angelou's role as an activist who fearlessly took on not only the white establishment but also the black bourgeoisie, I relished this moment. I knew this young man was about to get his comeuppance. It was just a matter of how she would deliver the knock-out punch.

I shouldn't have been surprised when I saw there was no punch at all. Dr. Angelou wasn't in the least per-turbed. Her response was not only measured, it was also respectful. And not only respectful, but also loving.

"I see you have studied our culture," she said, "and for that, dear brother, I commend you. The history of how black people survived the stranglehold of American society is deep and complex. You have your point of view. I understand how, by watching certain films and digesting certain images, you came to your conclusion. I could speak on the subject for many hours. I could direct you to many theories and discuss many ways to delineate the phenomenon that you find so disagreeable. But in-stead of using logic, argument, or analysis to drive home my position, I wonder if you would allow me to read from a poem I wrote some thirty years ago. I trust I'm not being self-indulgent by citing this old verse of mine.

It's simply that these lines of poetry best convey everything I feel about the many cogent points that you made. I call the poem 'Song for the Old Ones.'"

As Dr. Angelou recited from memory, her voice had never sounded more mellifluous. She spoke slowly, gracing each word with loving attention:

My Fathers sit on benches
  their flesh counts every plank
  the slats leave dents of darkness
deep in their withered flanks.

They nod like broken candles
  all waxed and burnt profound
  they say "It's understanding
that makes the world go round."

There in those pleated faces
  I see the auction block
  the chains and slavery's coffles
the whip and lash and stock.

My Fathers speak in voices
  that shred my fact and sound
  they say "It's our submission
that makes the world go round."

They used the finest cunning
 their naked wits and wiles
 the lowly Uncle Tomming
and Aunt Jemima's smiles.

They've laughed to shield their crying
 then shuffled through their dreams
 and stepped 'n' fetched a country
to write the blues with screams.

I understand their meaning
 it could and did derive
 from living on the edge of death
They kept my race alive.

When she was through, you could hear a pin drop. I looked at the young man who had provoked her recital and thought I saw tears in his eyes. After a few seconds of silence, the room exploded in thunderous applause. When my gaze returned to Dr. Angelou, I saw tears in her eyes as well. If I hadn't restrained myself, I would have been weeping.

It was because of Dr. Angelou's remarkable ability to transform what would have been a heated argument into healing art that we were all so moved.

*   *   *

We had been in Accra for a full week. There was great anticipation about Dr. Angelou's speech—her tribute to W. E. B. Du Bois—scheduled to be the final event of our trip. The evening before, she was being honored at a reception at the Osu Castle, a sprawling and majestic white edifice that sits atop a cliff overlooking the Atlantic Ocean. It is an elaborate colonial structure built by the Danes in the seventeenth century that belonged to many occupying powers, including Portugal and England, until the Ghanaians claimed it for themselves in the modern era of independence. At the time we were there, it served as a presidential residence.

Because it was known to have been a center of the West African slave trade, I felt a foreboding air about the enormous building. There are dungeons, which we were not shown, that held human beings before they were shipped off to foreign lands and lives of enslavement.

The large reception room into which we were ushered was nicely appointed and bore no suggestion of the castle's horrific history. The guests surrounding Dr. Angelou were local dignitaries eager to shake her hand. It was a pleasant and uneventful occasion until, much to my amazement, Stokely Carmichael made an appearance along with Miriam Makeba. They both seemed well acquainted with practically everyone, especially Dr. Angelou. Carmichael and Makeba had come to Ghana to hear her speech about Du Bois.

Makeba, of course, was an acclaimed artist, loved the world over as Mama Africa. Born in the townships of Johannesburg, she had long fought against apartheid. Because the South African government had revoked her passport in 1960, she had lived in exile until 1990. Now, in the summer of 1993, we were only months away from the historic moment when Nelson Mandela would win the presidency—in the spring of 1994—and, once and for all, end apartheid.

Carmichael, who led the black power movement in the 1960s and had challenged Dr. King for the leadership of black America, had changed his name to Kwame Ture and had been living in Africa for twenty-four years.

My mind raced back to my reading about the civil rights movement. I remembered the historic antiwar march in April of 1967, at which both he and Dr. King were present. Despite Dr. King's usual brilliance, it was Stokely who captured the moment with an incendiary address before a crowd of 125,000 protesters on the streets of New York. That was the day he spoke of how America had been built on genocide.

A fervent pan-Africanist, he left the United States and became embroiled in the complex politics of Guinea. Some thought that, given the inscrutable labyrinth that was African government at the time, he had lost his bearings. But that night in Accra he did not seem lost at all. He was a tall, handsome man dressed in multicolored African garb; his hair had turned gray, and his demeanor seemed softer than it had been in the United States. Nonetheless, he stood erect and exuded notable self-confidence. At fifty-two, he had retained his charisma. He received as much attention as Dr. Angelou.

Later that evening, Dr. Angelou was kind enough to introduce us. I did little more than shake his hand. Seeing that I couldn't contribute to the lively conversation he was having with Dr. Angelou, I was content to listen. They spoke lovingly of Kwame Nkrumah, who, I learned, had been one of Carmichael's main mentors when he arrived in Africa in the late 1960s.

After he and Dr. Angelou had spoken, Stokely was approached by several African men who took issue with some of his recent stances. These were Ghanaian officials and university professors of political science. An agile debater, Stokely more than held his own against accusations that his militancy had been misplaced in his support of certain regimes.

When the debate heated up, I wondered whether Dr. Angelou, who was especially knowledgeable about African politics, would enter the fray. She did not. When the spirited exchange finally wound down, I heard her tell him, "It's so wonderful to see you, my brother. So wonderful to see that you're still engaged in the work that speaks to your heart."

She wasn't as interested in questioning the nuances of his politics as she was in recognizing his humanity. Like her, he was an independent thinker committed to telling the truth as he saw it. She saw him—as she saw so many diverse people from so many diverse backgrounds—as family. If she was convinced he had made a mistake in political judgment, this was neither the time nor place to criticize. This was the time to reassert her love and appreciation for a brother who, like her, was still fighting the good fight.

The trip's main event unfolded the next day at what was officially called the W. E. B. Du Bois Memorial Centre for Pan-African Culture. It was here that Dr. Angelou delivered her major address.

The center itself is a single-story home where Du Bois had lived with his wife, Shirley. Its modesty is striking. Inside, in his bedroom and personal study, are many of his degrees as well as the caps and gowns he had worn to graduation ceremonies. I took note of one parchment that indicated he had received a bachelor of arts from Harvard in 1890. Atop a memorial outside the building is a bust of his head, tilted upward. Among the many plaques on the property is one that carries this quotation from Du Bois carved in granite: "One thing alone I charge you. As you live, believe in life. Always human beings will live and progress to greater, broader and fuller life. The only possible death is to lose belief in this truth simply because the great end comes slowly, because time is long."

Inside, forty or fifty people had crowded into a reception room, where we sat on wooden chairs facing a lectern. Among us were photographers and reporters from the international media. Kwame Ture—Stokely Carmichael—was seated in the front row. I took a seat in the back row but made sure to get a clear view of the speaker. Dr. Angelou was glowing. She looked elegant in a blue polka-dot suit and white blouse. Even before she began to speak, I felt the spirit of W. E. B. Du Bois. It was as though he were standing next to her in this old house of his.

Graciously, she introduced the dignitaries who were present—Jerry John Rawlings, president of Ghana; Kwame Ture; and many others. She expressed her gratitude for the privilege of speaking about a man she so deeply admired.

"Let me start on a personal note," she said. "As many of you know, I was brought up in a strictly segregated hamlet in Arkansas. That was during the Great Depression. The black school I attended had few books and fewer still that listed the accomplishments of people of color. Because I was both a precocious and voracious reader, I made it my business to get hold of books that would feed my hungry soul. That took enormous effort on my part. The efforts paid off. As a teenager, I began to read about how W. E. B. Du Bois had challenged the ideas of Booker T. Washington, who had been held up to us as something of a god. My friends, I didn't even know what it meant for one thinker to challenge another. Yet when I read *The Souls of Black Folk,* I immediately understood. Dr. Du Bois was challenging me—and, as a result, I was thrilled. I read everything I could about him. He was the first intellectual to enter my life. Because he was black, and because he wrote about blackness, I related to every word.

"Well, a year or so later I moved to California to be with my mother. It was there, in San Francisco, where I received a college scholarship. This was heady stuff for a young girl straight off the farm. Then came the day when I learned the college had invited Dr. Du Bois to speak. Naturally I was over the moon. I would get to see my hero in the flesh. I arrived at the lecture early, to be certain to find a seat. That's when I was shocked. Aside from myself and perhaps two or three others, everyone was white.

"Good Lord! I thought to myself. White people attending a lecture at a white college are surely expecting a white lecturer. When they see that Dr. Du Bois is black, they will get up and leave. And if they leave, he'll leave, and I'll never get to hear him speak. I must warn him! But before I could do a thing, the great man himself arrived. Just as I expected, the minute he entered the hall, the audience rose. But then, much to my shock and delight, they did not leave. They gave him a standing ovation before he uttered a single word. I knew I was witnessing a scene that I would never forget.

"So memorable was this scene from my young womanhood that when I came to Ghana some thirty years ago, I had every intention of telling the story to Dr. Du Bois in person. Unfortunately, my stay in Accra coincided with a decline in his health. I knew this because his wife, Shirley, and I became friends. She knew how much I wanted to meet her husband, and one day she graciously invited me to lunch. I'd finally get to meet my hero! But unfortunately he wasn't feeling well that day and was confined to his bedroom. After lunch, though, he did come out to say hello. I was elated. Although he was terribly frail—he was, after all, ninety-five—his eyes were alert. He sat next to me and took my hand. He understood this moment. When I told him my story about attending his lecture in San Francisco and worrying that the white audience would run out once they discovered he was black, he laughed heartily. That laugh meant the world to me. On that afternoon, right here in this very house, I was able tell W. E. B. Du Bois how much I admired him. I was able to tell him how his mind—his writings, his analyses, his aspirations, his political astuteness, his psychological insights, his intellectual bravery and originality—had influenced me.

"I related to Dr. Du Bois not only because of the clarity of his thought but also because of the way he inserted the lyrics of hymns, spirituals, and slave songs into his text. His words sang. His writing was musical. The music generated by Dr. Du Bois was the same passionate music I had heard in my grandmother's country church in Stamps, Arkansas. Yes, his thought was elevated, but its elevation came on the wings of lyrical fancy. He quoted from the Song of Solomon—'I am black, but comely, O ye daughters of Jerusalem.' He quoted the poetry of Alfred, Lord Tennyson. He quoted Elizabeth Barrett Browning. He quoted an old Negro song: 'I walk through the churchyard / To lay this body down; / I know moon-rise, I know star-rise; / I walk in the moonlight, I walk in the starlight; / I'll lie in the grave and stretch out my arms, / I'll go to judgment in the evening of the day, / And my soul and thy soul shall meet that day, / When I lay this body down.'

"He taught me that poetry and song and deep thinking are all cut from the same cloth. The mere title of his tome touched my heart. Think of it. Calling a groundbreaking sociological study *The Souls of Black Folk* revealed the sweetness of his own soul. He saw us not as some ethnic group but as his brothers and sisters. He saw us as folk—*his* folk. He did not focus on some cold, clinical analysis. He focused on our very souls. He underscored our humanity.

"And of course he saw us as no writer had seen us before. He wrote of the 'peculiar sensation' of living life with a double consciousness. I love how he put it, how he described—and I quote—'this sense of always looking at one's self through the eyes of others, of measuring one's soul by the tape of a world that looks on in amused contempt and pity. One ever feels his twoness— an American, a Negro; two souls, two thoughts, two unreconciled strivings; two warring ideals in one dark body, whose dogged strength alone keeps it from being torn asunder.'

"What was beautiful about Dr. Du Bois was his ability to allow paradox to live and breathe its own complex life. He never shied away from the contradictions of being black in America. He never reduced confusion into clichés. He let confusion stand. He understood the mighty challenge of being what he called 'a coworker in

the kingdom of culture, to escape both death and iso-
lation, and to husband and use his best powers and his
latent genius. These powers of body and mind have in
the past been strangely wasted, dispersed, or forgotten.'
From there he took us back through history, through
Egypt and Ethiopia, and the remarkable accomplishments of black civilization.

"It is still difficult to fathom the fact that his book
was published in 1903—ninety years ago. At the start of
the new millennium, he wrote these prophetic words: 'I
have seen a land right merry with the sun, where children
sing, and rolling hills lie like passioned women wanton
with harvest. And there in the King's Highways sat and
sits a figure veiled and bowed, by which the traveler's
footsteps hasten as they go. On the tainted air broods
fear. Three centuries' thought has been the raising and
unveiling of that bowed human heart, and now behold a
century new for the duty and the deed. The problem of
the twentieth century is the problem of the color line.'

"As we approach the end of that century, the relevance
of his statement has only grown. For all our so-called
progress, the problem remains the same. That fact—especially as it exists in the United States—astounds me.
It astounds me because we have already been paid for.
We have endured the unspeakable conditions of the Middle Passage, where we were chained to one another, sick-

ened by our own feces and urine and menstrual blood, squeezed next to the corpses of those whose beaten bodies could take no more. Yes, we have been paid for, my friends. Paid for by landowners who whipped our men into brutal submission, who pitilessly raped our women, who separated us from our children, who destroyed our families, who mounted an unholy campaign of terror—of decades of public lynchings—calculated to imprison us in fear, rob us of all dignity, and steal our very humanity. Yes, Lord, we have been paid for!

"And yet we owe a debt that we can never fully repay—a debt to intellectual and moral geniuses like Dr. Du Bois, who taught us that it is our spirit that can never die. It is our unbreakable spirit that defies darkness and death itself. It is our spirit that keeps us strong, sees us through, and, finally, gloriously turns wrong to right."

She continued her loving tribute to Du Bois in an address that lasted the better part of an hour. Again and again, she returned to his own words, reciting them with inspired grace. She said that, in challenging Booker T. Washington's policy of accommodation, Du Bois argued that "the hushing of criticism of honest opponents is a dangerous thing. It leads some of the best of the critics to unfortunate silence and paralysis of effort, and others to burst into speech so passionately and intemperately as to lose listeners."

Dr. Angelou never lost her listeners, not for a second. She carried on the noble tradition of the man whose eloquence she brilliantly reflected. She spoke with a beguiling mixture of muscularity and delicacy. Her prose carried the lilting quality of poetry. She praised Du Bois for his recommitment to the act of praise itself. She ended with a hymn that projected the determined hope at the heart of Du Bois's teaching:

I'll tell of the pit, with its gloom and despair,
I'll praise the dear Father, who answered my prayer;
I'll sing my new song, the glad story of love,
Then join in the chorus with the saints above.

What would top that? After her lecture, we were back at the presidential palace for a late-night snack.

"Let's sit together for a few seconds," she said. "We have an arduous trip ahead of us tomorrow. A few seconds of reflection would do us both good."

"It's an experience I'll never forget," I was quick to say.

"I'm glad to hear that, young Tavis Smiley. Your enthusiasm has been an unexpected blessing. Now, however, we face the time-old challenge that comes from extensive traveling. You've probably faced this challenge before."

"I'm not sure," I said. "I haven't done much traveling."

"The challenge centers on reentry. After an exhilarating trip like this to a foreign and exotic land, how do we reenter the life that we left behind?"

"To be truthful, Dr. Angelou, when I was offered the chance to come on this trip, I left that life with great eagerness."

She gently asked me, "Why is that, Tavis?"

"I had suffered a crushing defeat."

"Tell me about it."

I appreciated Dr. Angelou's interest and answered the question in depth, describing my desire to be a public servant, my entry into the city council race, and the disheartening results. I explained that, before boarding the plane for Ghana, I had felt a sharp sense of rejection.

"Perhaps because of my long history as a dancer, actress, and writer, rejection is something with which I am all too familiar," she said.

"Your accomplishments in those fields, though, are legendary."

"Yes, but for every accomplishment there were twenty rejections. A dance company thought my style was incompatible with theirs. A casting director found me lacking. An editor considered my writing too fanciful, or too plain, or too abstract or concrete. I could go on for hours. In the end, though, only one attitude enabled me to move ahead. That attitude said, 'Rejection can simply mean redirection.' To cite an example from your life, Tavis, you could easily postulate that without the rejection you experienced at the polls, you would not have been redirected to Accra. Do you find my reasoning at all plausible?"

"I do."

"Well, if that's the case, then it's not silly to see rejection as a gift whose contents and character may not be known until a later time. But that doesn't mean that the gift isn't real. It doesn't mean that the gift isn't precious. And it doesn't mean that the gift isn't helping us to subtly shift our thinking from willful expectation to grateful acceptance. We want our journey to be directed by God, not our adamant insistence that things go our way."

"I may be guilty of that very tendency," I said.

"We all are. Human nature. All we can do is be more aware. I try to stay alert to the possibility that after an exciting trip such as this, coming home to our old routine may be a letdown. We need a reentry strategy."

"How would you describe the strategy?"

"Awareness that life has its highs and lows. This trip was a high. If we encounter a low afterward, we shouldn't be surprised. We should be ready. When we eliminate the element of surprise, the low has less of a hold on us. That's because we're already looking for it. It's something like that beautiful old song Billie Holiday used to sing—the same Billie Holiday, bless her heart, who told me that I'd never make my fortune as a singer. That's the song called 'Good Morning, Heartache,' in which she has a perfectly reasonable dialogue with heartache."

In a blues-tinted voice, Dr. Angelou sang the words: "'Might as well get used to you hanging around / Good morning, heartache, sit down.'"

"It's the blues," I said. "You're saying when I get home the blues might be waiting for me."

"The blues are never very far from our door. The blues are the mark of our human condition. But you and I know that the blues—those low-down, dirty blues—can be beautiful. Not to mention transformative."

To view rejection as redirection really is transformative, I had to admit.

"All part of our glorious journey, young Tavis Smiley. I know you remember that song the saints used to sing." Suddenly she broke into a song:

On my journey now, Mount Zion...

One day I was walking along,
Well, the elements opened
And the love came down...

I went to the valley, and I didn't go to stay,
Well, my soul got happy
And I stayed all day...

You can talk about me
Just as much as you please...
But the more you talk
I'm gonna stay on my knees...

The song was over.

Tomorrow the trip would be over.

A few hours later, my bags were packed.

On the long flight home, I kept hearing Dr. Angelou's voice. It was a voice that I had come to know and love.

In the middle of the night, heading home to a future that was unknown and a little scary, I kept asking myself a question that, even with all her wisdom, Dr. Angelou could not answer. It was something I needed to answer on my own.

When would I find my voice?

PART TWO

Voices

6

Reentry

It took me months to unpack the thoughts and feelings I experienced during my trip to Ghana. Emotionally, it had been the heaviest journey of my adult life.

In my mind, I kept replaying my conversations with Dr. Angelou, kept rereading the copious notes I made on her remarks, kept reminding myself of the comfort that her voice provided. Her voice was more than mellow; it was musical, nuanced, dramatic, warm, and inquisitive; it was endlessly enthralling.

And it was not only Dr. Angelou's voice that continued to resonate inside my head. With new clarity I heard the people of whom she had spoken with a sense of urgency.

I heard Dr. King. I heard Malcolm X. I heard Stokely Carmichael. I heard W. E. B. Du Bois.

Each had a powerful and distinctive voice. Each had something vital to say. Each exuded strength and certitude. Each revealed a depth of conviction.

Dr. Angelou had warned me about the dangers of comparison. She said to compare is to create a winner-loser dynamic in which I'd wind up a loser. She urged me to view people I admired in their full humanity, not as faultless icons. I heard that as sound advice, but I was having a hard time applying it. What I really wanted to do was to pick up the phone and call Dr. Angelou. Since she had brought up the subject of comparisons and warned me of the difficulty of reentry, she'd be the perfect person to consult.

But how could I do that?

Sure, we had spoken at length in Ghana. And sure, she had said nice things about me. But that was then and this was now. I was an acquaintance of hers, not a friend. I did not believe that I had established or earned the rapport that would allow me to call her. Besides, I hadn't asked for her contact information, and she hadn't offered it.

I thought of calling Julianne Malveaux to get Dr. Angelou's number, but what would be the point? I did not want to appear presumptuous or pushy. I couldn't leapfrog over the Malveaux-Maya relationship and assume that I had carte blanche. Besides, what was it that I wanted Dr. Angelou to say that she hadn't already told me? In my mind, she had given me more attention than I deserved.

What did I really want? In truth, I wanted her to hold my hand, to walk me through my own next steps. But I could hardly express that thought to myself, much less to her.

And I wanted again to hear her voice. I satisfied that yearning by turning to her books, a place where her voice came through loud and clear. I went back to *I Know Why the Caged Bird Sings*. In this, the first of her many memoirs, she tells what has become a famous story—perhaps the central story in her life.

After she left her grandmother's home in Stamps, Arkansas, to be with her mother in Saint Louis, seven-year-old Maya was raped by her mother's boyfriend. The only person she told was her brother, Bailey, who in turn told the family. The rapist was put in jail for a night. When he was released, he was beaten to death. Maya thought it was her voice that had killed him—the voice that told the horrific news to her brother. For the next five and a half years she turned mute. She did not speak a word. Back in Stamps, she was comforted by poetry, especially Shakespeare, and especially Shakespeare's sonnet 29, which had her believing that Shakespeare must have been "a black girl in the South who had been molested." How else could he have written

> *When, in disgrace with fortune and men's eyes,*
> *I all alone beweep my outcast state,*
> *And trouble deaf heaven with my bootless cries,*
> *And look upon myself, and curse my fate,*
> *Wishing me like to one more rich in hope,*
> *Featur'd like him, like him with friends possess'd,*
> *Desiring this man's art and that man's scope,*
> *With what I most enjoy contented least;*
> *Yet in these thoughts myself almost despising,*
> *Haply I think on thee, and then my state,*
> *Like to the lark at break of day arising*
> *From sullen earth, sings hymns at heaven's gate;*
> > *For thy sweet love remember'd such wealth brings*
> > *That then I scorn to change my state with kings.*

It was only with the literary encouragement of Mrs. Flowers, an older black lady, that things began to change.

"You'll never really love poetry until you speak it," said Mrs. Flowers. "Until you feel it come across your tongue, over your teeth, and through your lips, you will never love poetry. Never."

For months Mrs. Flowers kept after young Maya.

Finally one fine morning she crept under the house, where, because of the scratching of the chickens, the dirt was soft. It was there where, for the first time in nearly six years, Maya spoke words. She recited poems and, in doing so, rediscovered her voice.

Because Dr. Angelou's writing is so vivid, I felt myself back there with her, traumatized in Saint Louis, struggling in Stamps, looking for a way back into the world. I related so strongly because I had suffered a trauma of my own. When I thought of the beating that had been unleashed on my sister and me when I was in seventh grade, I remembered that afterward I, too, felt as though I had lost my voice.

In reliving this memory, my first instinct was to say—as I said to Dr. Angelou in Ghana—that my ordeal was nothing compared with hers. But I remembered her admonition about comparisons and resisted the temptation to belittle my experience.

That experience did turn my world upside down. The state's Department of Child Services placed me in a home with foster parents. After four months away from my family, I missed my siblings and went back home. But I remained hurt, confused, and furious about what had happened to me. I thought of the phrase I had read in 2 Chronicles: "A rage that reacheth up unto heaven."

When my parents spoke to me, I answered mono-syllabically. *Yes, ma'am. No, sir.* Short responses that conveyed the fury beneath my passive aggression.

I recovered my voice only when I entered speech tour-naments in which I delivered the major addresses of Dr. King. I borrowed his voice and, as a result, became a consistent winner.

Then came the day when my parents caught me in a lie. I had told them I was practicing for a tournament when in fact I had been rehearsing with a singing group at school. Even though we were harmonizing to songs like "What the World Needs Now Is Love," my mother had forbidden secular singing of any kind. As a result, I was prohibited from participating in speech tournaments for the next three weeks. That meant I'd miss out on two chances for first-place ribbons. The more ribbons, the greater my chance to win the all-state competition. I just had to win all-state.

I pleaded to no avail. Their decision was final.

More than ever, my voice was muted. It took months to regain my voice and even longer to reconcile with my parents.

In 1994, the year after I returned from Ghana, I turned thirty. It was time to face facts. I needed work. But I was still determined to find a way into public service, still looking for a job that would allow me to serve in the spirit of Dr. King—a job where I could make a real difference. No such job existed, so I decided to invent one. Out of pure necessity, I found a way to develop my own voice, since I was already quite comfortable speaking publicly from my days in Mayor Bradley's office.

I say "necessity" because the job was radio commentary. The very essence of the job was that I speak my mind and heart.

I started slowly. By landing my own sponsor, I was able to do a one-minute commentary called "Just a Thought" on local AM radio in LA. I spoke about everything from gun control to immigration. It turned out that radio was the perfect outlet for me, allowing me to express myself and grow my confidence. Stevie Wonder heard me and put me on the FM station he owned. From there I went to a megastation called The Beat. Next thing I knew, the local ABC affiliate, KABC-TV, asked me to do my commentary on their five o'clock evening news. I declined, only because I knew that I needed to hone my TV skills. So I went to Montreal for six months to woodshed on Canadian television. Back in LA, I reconnected with KABC and accepted their invitation. My commentaries were well received. The *Los Angeles Times* profiled me, and I and forty-nine others were part of a *Time* magazine cover story called "Fifty for the Future," an article about America's most promising leaders under the age of forty.

Compiling my commentaries, I self-published my first book, *Just a Thought*. Through my friend Ron Brown, President Clinton's secretary of commerce, I was asked to the White House to give black-media-outreach advice. That's where I met Tom Joyner, the nationally syndicated radio personality. Tom and I partnered, and, for a dozen years, I did regular commentaries on his highly rated morning show. He and I tackled tough issues. In one historic instance, we were able to persuade advertisers to stop the discriminatory practice of refusing to advertise on black media.

The next step was a big one. BET contacted me in September of 1996 about a nightly talk show to be broadcast live from Washington, DC. They were casting around for hosts. Each candidate—everyone from to Snoop Dogg to Ice-T—was to be given a weeklong trial run. No one wanted to go first. I wasn't sure I wanted to go at all—I thought I was doing just fine in LA—but friends encouraged me, and I decided to take the plunge. I agreed to audition the first week. I flew to DC, where Whitney Houston was scheduled to be my guest. But the weekend before the show was to air, Tupac Shakur died. The plan immediately changed. My debut appearance as host of *BET Talk* would focus on the great rapper. I lined up Chuck D and hip-hop mogul Russell Simmons as guests.

I opened with commentary about Tupac's importance in our cultural history, followed by interviews with several of his colleagues. Russell, though, played hard to get. He had agreed to do a remote interview from our LA affiliate, but at the last minute, he decided he didn't want to go into the studio. He'd stay in his limo and call in from his cell phone. I had no choice but to put up a still photo of him as we spoke.

"Russell," I asked, "I wonder how much greater an artist Tupac could have become had he lived. I know he went through various stages of his career and life. Sometimes he was confused and conflicted. Given his genius for language, do you—"

Russell cut me off. "You house nigger."

"Excuse me?"

"You heard me. You're a house nigger. You know how many interviews I turned down today? I'm giving my only Tupac interview to BET 'cause I figure BET will honor him, and you start talking this stuff. You're a house nigger, and I'm done. I'm outta here."

Click.

All I could do was tell the audience that I was taking a break.

Back on the air, I said, "Welcome to the premiere of

BET Talk with, as Russell Simmons has characterized me, America's favorite house nigger."

In spite of my attempt to make light of the attack, I was devastated and did my best to get through the show.

Back in my hotel room, I considered my position. With four more shows to go, it was reasonable to assume that my chance of getting the gig was remote—especially after tonight's fiasco.

Then I started second-guessing myself. Had I been too complacent with Russell, too passive? Should I have fired back? Should I have defended myself? Or had there been some hidden hostility in my questions that I hadn't recognized? Was this disastrous interview in fact my fault? And, if so, what did that say about my ability to take on a job that, in all likelihood, would never be offered to me anyway?

That's when my phone rang.

"Is this young Tavis Smiley?"

I recognized her voice immediately. Who wouldn't?

Maya Angelou!

Since Ghana, almost three years earlier, I had only seen her once, and that was at the Million Man March, where she had read her poem "From a Black Woman to a Black Man," which ends with the wonderful lines, "The ancestors remind us, despite the history of pain / We are a going-on people who will rise again." I was covering the historic event as a broadcaster, and, given the whirlwind of activities, there was barely time for us to exchange warm greetings before she was ushered away.

That was a year ago. Now, for the first time, she was calling me on the phone.

"Dr. Angelou!" I exclaimed. "'How in the world did you find me?'"

"I have my sources."

"It's so good to hear your voice."

"I've been keeping track of you, baby. I've been listening to your commentaries."

"You have?"

"Indeed. And I'm pleased to see that you're fulfilling the promise I saw in you back in Ghana."

"I can't thank you enough, Dr. Angelou—"

"I know you were raised to respect your elders, Tavis, but this 'Dr. Angelou' business has gone far enough. At this point we can afford to be less formal."

"Well," I said, "I'm not sure what to call you. Is Sister Maya all right?"

"Sister?" she asked. "When I think of you, son, I think of myself more as a mother than a sister."

That statement melted my heart.

With some hesitation, I forced the words out of my mouth. "Mother Maya."

"Son," she said, "that sounds mighty good to me."

"You are the mother to many," I said.

"By design. It gives me great pleasure. It also gave me great pleasure to see you on the Black Entertainment Television network tonight."

"You watched the show?"

"Wouldn't have missed it for the world."

"I can't say I'm happy about it."

"I had a feeling you might be down. So I'm calling in hopes of lifting your spirit."

"You already have."

"You spoke of Tupac Shakur tonight," she said, "and you did so respectfully. Like all human beings, he is deserving of respect. Have I told you about my encounter with Tupac?"

"No," I said.

"When I first encountered him, I was on the set of *Poetic Justice,* the film in which director John Singleton asked me to make a cameo appearance. I was happy to do so. Janet Jackson was the star. I was in my trailer when I heard a ruckus outside. I looked out and saw two young black men reviling each other. The more aggressive of the two, a diminutive fellow with sparkling eyes, was cursing so vociferously I could practically see blue venom streaming from his mouth.

"Before the encounter turned violent, I approached him and said, 'May I speak to you for a moment?'

Surprised, he nonetheless continued to rant. 'This motherfu—'

" 'I understand,' I said, cutting off his tirade, 'but hear me out.'

"I walked him a few feet away from the man he was about to attack and said, 'When was the last time someone told you how important you are?'

"He had no answer, so I posed the question again.

" 'How long has it been, son, since another human being looked you in the eye and said that you were unique and precious?'

"He had no answer, but I had his attention. That's when I changed direction and spoke of other matters. I looked into those wide eyes of his and asked, 'Did you know that your ancestors were brought over in the filthy hatches of slave ships so you could stand here today? Did you know that they stood on auction blocks, where they were bought and sold like cattle?' I let those questions resonate for a few seconds before I went on. I spoke of history and heritage, of what we had been through as a people, and the miraculous manner in which we had clung to our dignity, our humanity, and our pride. He listened intently. Like butter in the sun, his animus melted. Now tears were streaming down his cheeks. As I put my arm around him, he openly wept. I escorted him back to his trailer, and when I returned to mine, Miss Janet Jackson was waiting for me.

" 'Do you know who you were talking to, Dr. Angelou?' she asked excitedly.

" 'I have no idea,' I said.

" 'That was Tupac Shakur.'

" 'Darling,' I said, 'I wouldn't know Tupac from a six-pack. To me, he was simply a young man in pain.'

"A week later I received a letter from his mother, Afeni. He had told her about our encounter, and she thanked me, saying that I may have saved his life. I wrote her back, saying that it had been a blessing for me. I simply saw him as a son who, at that moment, required a strong dose of love. Later, when I saw the depths of his great talent, I stood in admiration. And I told him so.

"What you said tonight about Tupac, Tavis, was undoubtedly the truth. You praised his genius for language. His poetry was born out of conflict and confusion. You offered no criticism but instead an honest tribute to a fallen brother. I heard the love in your voice."

"Russell Simmons certainly didn't."

"Mr. Simmons was merely trying to process the pain of losing Tupac. He transferred some of that pain onto you. Processing pain—without perpetuating pain—is rough business. Most of us don't do it well. But I thought you handled it respectfully. You avoided turning the pain back on him. You simply allowed it."

"And the insult to me?"

"In the long run, it will mean nothing, Tavis."

"He's hugely influential in the hip-hop community."

"Like all communities, the hip-hop community is highly diverse. Some will note the way in which he spoke to you. Most won't care. It will pass, but what will stay is your ability to stand on solid ground. To stand on your own. To accept whatever insults come your way—and believe me, as a public person, they will surely come—with a certain pluck combined with a steady serenity."

"I'm not sure I've found that serenity."

"You will, son," said Mother Maya. "It's only a matter of time. But for now, we can celebrate the fact that you have found what you have been looking for."

"And what's that?" I asked.

"Your voice," she answered. "And the way you found it was by realizing the greatest quality of all."

"Love?"

"No—courage."

"If I remember my Bible, it says, 'And now abide faith, hope, love, these three; but the greatest of these is love.'"

"Yet the greatest of the biblical characters—Abraham, Moses, Ruth, Solomon, David, Mary, and of course Jesus himself—exhibited towering courage. Without courage, love cannot be activated. It takes courage to love."

"But isn't the converse true, Mother Maya? Isn't it love that activates our courage? Isn't love the prime mover?"

"It's courageous of you to make your case, Tavis, but my life experience has me thinking otherwise. I *know* that courage is the core ingredient. Without it there is no creative life, no spiritual life. Without courage, life is bereft of excitement and wonder."

"I'm still sticking with love," I said. "It's love that got you to call me tonight. Courage had nothing to do with it."

"Not true. For all I knew, you'd be in no mood to talk to anyone. I needed courage to make the call."

"Nonsense! You knew I'd love hearing from you."

"Then I'm glad my courage allowed me to pick up the phone!"

"There's no winning!" I said with a laugh.

"There's *only* winning," Maya retorted. "The victory is there. All we have to do is claim it."

7

What's in a Name?

After Maya's first long-distance phone call, a warm acquaintance turned into a lasting friendship. I was finally able to speak to Maya as a colleague, not as a self-conscious intern. I had matured enough to embrace the maternal side of her character. And of course, it wasn't just me whom she saw as a son. In virtually all her relationships with young people, she viewed herself as a loving parent. We all were her sons and daughters, just as her contemporaries were her sisters and brothers. She looked at her vast network of friendships in strictly familial terms.

During our time in Ghana, I had been admitted

into her family. But my insecurities had been too great to accept the honor, to even realize it was happening. This time, though, I didn't hesitate in accepting Maya's support. It came at a critical juncture. It allowed me to complete that week as host of *BET Talk*. I brushed off the Russell Simmons confrontation and moved on. In the eyes of the network executives, I did well enough to earn an invitation for a second week of interviews. That led to a third, a fourth, and finally an offer to become the permanent host. No other candidates were auditioned.

The show was a solid hit. I was a nightly guest in the homes of millions of television watchers. Much to my amazement, I became a household name in black America.

My first book from a major publisher was *Hard Left,* essays on my belief that hysteria from the political right was drowning out this country's reasonable voices. I made certain that my promotional tour included a stop at Special Occasions, a black bookstore in Winston-Salem, North Carolina, where Maya maintained her central residence while she was professor of American studies at Wake Forest University.

She had told me the story of how, upon her first visit to campus in the early 1970s, she had accepted an invitation to entertain student questions after her formal lecture. The informal sessions lasted past midnight.

"That's when I realized what I had been missing," she said. "The students had such fresh vitality, such a keen hunger for learning and sharing information, that I knew one day I'd have to come back."

When she came back, in 1982, she was named the university's first Reynolds Professor of American Studies and given carte blanche to teach whatever she liked.

"I wound up teaching everything from the literature of the American South to the poetry of Shakespeare," she said. "Before it all began, I saw myself as a writer dabbling in teaching. But once in the classroom, I realized that I was essentially a teacher dabbling in writing. That's how exciting it was."

Two weeks before arriving in Winston-Salem, I had called Maya, hoping I could see her during my stopover.

"I'd make a fabulous feast for you," she said. "I'd invite you as my houseguest. You'd be welcome for as long as you like, but unfortunately you're coming at a time when I'll be out of the city."

I was disappointed but heartened when she gave me a rain check. I looked forward to returning and staying at her home.

When I got to Special Occasions, I was doubly heartened when the owner told me that Maya had bought a whole box of my books and asked that I autograph each one. She planned on giving them to her closest friends.

That's why I was a little surprised when, after I got back to LA, Maya called to say she had a reservation about the book.

"Not the writing," she said. "The writing is clear, and your ideas are set forth with logic and passion. It's the title that bothers me, young Tavis Smiley."

"The play on words?"

"Playing with words is fine. Puns are fun. There's nothing wrong with a good ol' double entendre. It isn't the pun I object to: it's the word *hard*."

"That's how I felt, Mother Maya. I wanted to make my position known."

"But at what cost, son? At the cost of alienating those who may well be put off by the title's tone? If you're only interested in preaching to the choir, that's one thing. Then yes, your title can openly announce your adamancy. But if I know you at all, Tavis, I know you as a man interested in reaching as many people as possible. In my mind, you don't do that by advertising a hard-and-fast position. You do that through invitation. The invitation might be gentle. It might be tantalizing. It might be provocative. But whatever it is, it should not set up a resistance. It should not shout, 'Here I am! If you're with me, line up behind me. If not, get lost.'"

"I'm not sure I agree."

"I suspected that. Why else would you choose that title?"

I laughed. Maya always came on strong, but never in a way that discouraged dissent.

"I chose the title," I said, "because it was apt. I felt the need to state my case with force. I'm not sure the forcefulness of my title is any more adamant than the forcefulness of your argument against it."

Now it was Maya's turn to laugh.

"You're saying that I'm taking a *hard* position against your *Hard Left*?" she said. "Is that it?"

"That's it exactly."

"Well, then I must soften my approach. I must say, my dear son, that it was with great pride that I received your text. In it I saw the blossoming of a mind. Yet the verbal ribbon atop this literary package did not seem to match its content. It was as though the contents were painted in a pleasing shade of azure blue while the ribbon was a shocking shade of chartreuse."

"But if the chartreuse caught your attention, perhaps that was what motivated you to look inside."

"And so we come to the law of diminishing returns."

"How is that?" I asked.

"In disagreements such as these, friends can banter back and forth. That can be enlightening and even fun. Every now and then I enjoy a good intellectual jostle.

But at a certain point push comes to shove. The wise person—and believe me, that wise person is not always me—will recognize that point. The wise person will see that further dispute will only lead to frustration and aggravation. The core of the argument is suddenly overwhelmed by the demands of the ego. The ego says, 'I will not let go. I cannot let go. I must be right.' If we heed the ego, the combat becomes brutal, and pride, rather than understanding, rules the day. It isn't differences of opinion that ruin friendships. It's pride. And what is pride if not a puffed-up sense of self?"

"So what am I supposed to do with all the many justifications for my title? As you've been talking, I've been building them up in my mind. I suppose I should just drop them and tell you that I love you for all the attention you lavish on me."

Maya laughed. "Yes, that sounds good. And I must return that love for all the attention you lavish on me."

"This is a good lesson learned. If I write another book, before I do anything, I need to consult Maya on the title."

"And if you catch me on a good day, I hope to have the serenity to tell you, 'Tavis, it's your book, and it must be your title.'"

"So you'll let me make another mistake."

"The lesson learned—as you put it—is that perhaps

there are no mistakes. Just steps along the way. If we stumble, we get up and keep steppin'."

"You took a big step with the title of your first book. It couldn't have been more perfect."

"And it didn't come from me. It came from Paul Laurence Dunbar, who wrote the lines in his poem 'Sympathy' back in the nineteenth century."

Without warning, Maya broke into a dramatic rendition of the poem. Her recitation had all the majestic rhythm of a spiritual.

I know what the caged bird feels, alas!
When the sun is bright on the upland slopes;
When the wind stirs soft through the springing grass,
And the river flows like a stream of glass;
When the first bird sings and the first bud opes,
And the faint perfume from its chalice steals—
I know what the caged bird feels!

I know why the caged bird beats his wing
Till its blood is red on the cruel bars;
For he must fly back to his perch and cling
When he fain would be on the bough a-swing;
And a pain still throbs in the old, old scars
And they pulse again with a keener sting—
I know why he beats his wing!

I know why the caged bird sings, ah me,
* When his wing is bruised and his bosom sore,—*
When he beats his bars and he would be free;
It is not a carol of joy or glee,
* But a prayer that he sends from his heart's deep core,*
But a plea, that upward to Heaven he flings—
I know why the caged bird sings!

"That was a treat," I said. "Do you always memorize poetry in its entirety?"

"I do when I love the poem. And this was a poem I adored. Yet it didn't occur to me to borrow its signature line for my book. The idea came from my dear friend the jazz singer Abbey Lincoln. She had read my manuscript and told me that she thought the sentiment fit."

"And I'll ask what you've been asked a thousand times before. Why do you think it fits?"

"Why do *you* think it fits, Tavis?"

"A soaring spirit cannot be contained."

"As good an answer as any!"

"But is it the right answer?" I asked.

"If it works for you, it works for me. I've entertained hundreds of such answers and, to be truthful, I'm grateful for all of them. To have written a book that inspires personal response from a multitude of people is reward unto itself. Though they express it in different ways, most everyone understands the underlying feeling that you just articulated, Tavis. Most everyone realizes that the caged bird sings because song is embedded within her soul. She sings because she must. She sings because she was made to sing. She sings because singing is her gift and her joy. Circumstances may suppress us. Circumstances may even imprison us. But our essential song— that spirit that lets us soar beyond our bodies and surpass the limitations of our surroundings—that song is one that will always be sung."

8

What's in a Word?

Maya did nothing with only half a heart—including cook. Her beautiful cooking was legendary, so when I was traveling the East Coast later that year, I cashed in my rain check and accepted Maya's invitation to visit her home in Winston-Salem, North Carolina.

"I'll have that fabulous dinner party I promised," she said. "You'll meet some of my friends here. And you'll stay over, so we'll have lots of time to talk."

I felt terrific as Maya greeted me at the front porch of her spacious home on Bartram Road. The exterior was painted a friendly yellow. The interior was all soft chairs and cozy couches. She took me on a tour and pointed out the paintings by Romare Bearden, John Biggers, and Charles White. African and African American art was everywhere.

"I know it might seem somewhat prideful to display a portrait of myself," she said, indicating a painting by David Sugar, "but I simply had to hang this one. When I look at it, I see my grandmother. I'm proud to say that I grew up to look like her."

Her sun-filled library was lined from floor to ceiling with books, and there were cozy corners in which to discuss them. But the best discussions happened in the eating area next to her expansive kitchen.

Beyond the gate leading to the backyard was a six-foot-tall blue birdcage. Surrounding the stand-alone guest cottage were eight more birdcages.

"I know why the writer has birdcages," I said.

"These are happy birds. They sing night and day. Come, let's stroll through the garden."

There, among the fragrant flowers and blooming plants, Maya had placed some of the awards she had received. They were many, including those in the name of Mahatma Gandhi, Martin Luther King Jr., Rosa Parks, Nelson Mandela, and Malcolm X, whose images were rendered in busts raised on small pedestals.

Back in the house, she fixed me a delicious lunch.

"We're going vegetarian today, my dear Tavis," she

said. "I'm serving you my famous pressed leek, asparagus, and zucchini terrine with a mustard-lemon dressing. As I approach seventy, I'm cooking with a lighter touch."

"Have you turned vegetarian entirely?" I asked.

"No, though my dear friend Nick Ashford is a hardcore vegetarian. His lovely wife, Valerie Simpson, is somewhat less orthodox. Together, they've motivated me to cook in a less meaty style. Which reminds me—have I told you about my early brush with vegetarianism when I was living out in Los Angeles?"

I had to hear the story—even *that* one was going to be interesting in her hands.

"I love telling the story. One day I walked into an establishment known as Ye Olde Health Food Diner. This was thirty years ago, when LA was the capital of vegetarianism. I was not only a committed meat eater but also a smoker. A few years later I would quit tobacco, never to return. It was a habit I was glad to renounce. On this particular morning, though, I was smoking as I entered the establishment. In those days you could still light up in restaurants. But the horrified waitress, a notably officious woman, said, 'No, no, no—not in here.' I quickly snuffed out my cigarette, took my seat, and ordered veggies and rice. Looking around, I noticed that all the customers looked pale and sickly.

"'I'm guessing these people, like me, are here for the

first time,' I told my waitress. 'They must be coming here to eat healthier and get better.'

" 'Oh, no,' the waitress responded. 'They're all vegetarians. They've been coming around here for years.'

" 'If I were you,' I said, 'I'd keep that to myself.'

"The waitress didn't laugh. And my veggies and rice didn't have any taste. So I hurried and wrote a poem I called 'The Health-Food Diner.' May I share it with you?"

"Of course."

Maya then recited her poem with her trademark dramatic flair:

No sprouted wheat and soya shoots
And Brussels in a cake,
Carrot straw and spinach raw,
(Today, I need a steak).

Not thick brown rice and rice pilaw
Or mushrooms creamed on toast,
Turnips mashed and parsnips hashed,
(I'm dreaming of a roast).

Health-food folks around the world
Are thinned by anxious zeal,
They look for help in seafood kelp
(I count on breaded veal).

What's in a Word?

No smoking signs, raw mustard greens,
Zucchini by the ton,
Uncooked kale and bodies frail
Are sure to make me run

to

Loins of pork and chicken thighs
And standing rib, so prime,
Pork chops brown and fresh ground round
(I crave them all the time).

Irish stews and boiled corned beef
and hot dogs by the scores,
or any place that saves a space
For smoking carnivores.

I applauded enthusiastically.

That evening Maya made good on her promise and put together an extravagant dinner party for ten. The guests were friends and associates. Some were professors from Wake Forest, others were writers and artists who lived in the area. Maya took pride not only in preparing a scrumptious five-course meal but also in setting the table with exquisite taste. The linen tablecloth, the silverware, the fine china, the ivory-colored napkins folded in the shapes of blossoms, the fresh flowers, the vintage wine—everything was just so.

Seated at the head of the table, Maya was a model hostess. Without dominating the discourse, she kept the conversation moving—never allowing it to lag yet never rushing it along. She was careful to make certain each of her guests received a good share of attention. She spoke of their past accomplishments and asked about their present activities. If someone was shy, Maya didn't press. Her extreme sensitivity was something to behold.

The conversation was lively, and the subjects ranged from politics to poetry to a bit of local gossip. There was an easy exchange of views. I suspected the other guests felt much the way I did. We were privileged to be seated at Maya's table.

It was no secret that Maya liked to drink. The subject came up during dinner, when one of the guests asked about her custom of working on books in hotel rooms.

"I heard that you like to steal away with simply a yellow pad, a pen, and a glass of sherry by your side," said the guest.

"Oh, no, dear," Maya responded. "Not a glass of sherry. A bottle."

I never saw Maya overdo it. She was the model of restraint. But neither did she deny the pleasure she derived from fine wine. As the evening went on, she grew even more gregarious. Drinking seemed to enhance her good cheer.

The same could not be said for one of her guests at a previous dinner party. Maya told us the story of this particular lady, who had been imbibing and was the only guest whose comments had gone against the grain of the otherwise harmonious conversation. During the first four courses, Maya ignored her—a telling sign that the train was going off the tracks.

Then came dessert—a luscious crème caramel. And that's when the subject turned to the political complexities of South Africa. The outspoken guest had once lived in Johannesburg and suddenly unleashed a torrent of opinions that could charitably be labeled as outrageous. It was an embarrassment. Maya began to seethe and wondered how she would respond. She told us you could cut the tension with a knife.

In the middle of her guest's tirade, Maya got up and walked over to the woman, who would not stop ranting.

With great equanimity, Maya said, "I have your purse, dear, and I'll have someone drive you home. Good evening."

The woman began to protest, but Maya cut her off.

"I'll have no such talk at my table. Not now. Not ever."

By taking charge and dismissing the woman out of hand, Maya had snuffed out the fire before it really started. She returned to a mood of great merriment, as though nothing had happened. Guests lingered long after dessert. Goodwill was restored. By evening's end, the incident was forgotten by the other guests. But the lesson stuck with all of us who were hearing it from Maya years later.

I awoke the following morning. I had only a few hours before my flight to New York. I followed the aroma of fresh butter biscuits to the kitchen, where Maya was busy cooking a bountiful breakfast.

"You're spoiling me," I said.

"You never know when friends may be sharing a last meal together. That's why each meal should be memorable."

Looking over at a pile of reading matter on the kitchen table, I said, "I see you've already been through the newspapers today. How many do you read?"

"I don't count. As many as interest me."

"And what interested you this morning?" I asked.

"An article about this being the fifth anniversary of Clarence Thomas's appointment to the Supreme Court."

I read over the article quickly and saw that it was highly critical of Thomas's ultraconservative stances.

The author also wondered why Thomas had yet to ask a single question to either a plaintiff or a defendant while hearing cases brought before the court. This was in 1996—and it's still big news if he does!

I was reminded, of course, of a famous op-ed piece Maya had written for the *New York Times* in 1991, when Thomas's nomination was the center of great controversy. The piece, which she called "I Dare to Hope," was a spirited defense of Thomas. It came at a time when Thomas was being lambasted for what liberals were calling his right-wing politics. He was also facing accusations of sexual harassment brought by Anita Hill, an African American attorney whom he had supervised at the Department of Education.

I was a little reluctant to say anything, because Maya's article was among the most controversial of her career.

"I sense a certain hesitancy on your part," said Maya, reading my mind. "Aren't you going to ask me anything about it?"

"About your original article arguing for Thomas?"

"Yes."

"Well," I said, "it was a bold piece."

"And..." she said, egging me on.

"And I thought you were dead wrong," I admitted.

Maya smiled. "I presumed that was your position."

"And I'm going to presume that what we've seen of Thomas's opinions in these five years is enough to make you change your mind."

"Your presumption is misplaced," she said as she set a plate of scrambled eggs and biscuits in front of me.

We said grace before resuming the discussion.

"Misplaced," I said, "because you still believe that you were right to support his nomination?"

"Yes. Even to the point that I'm including 'I Dare to Hope' in my new collection of essays, *Even the Stars Look Lonesome*."

"That's a beautiful title," I said. "But with all due respect, that's a very lonely position to cling to."

"You know me well enough, Tavis, to realize that being a solitary voice is of no concern to me."

"What's of concern to me, though, is that his opinions have hurt black people. His stance against affirmative action is enough to write him off as an adversary."

"He had a history as a conservative long before his nomination," said Maya. "That's why George Bush nominated him. You'll remember I acknowledged that in my article. I said that he has given his adversaries every reason to oppose and distrust him."

"And with all due respect, Maya, I contend that those of us who opposed and distrusted him were right to do so. His wrongheaded actions have proven us right."

"While you eat your eggs, let me go find my article. I want to remind myself—and you—just why I supported him. And why my support has not abated."

She went to her study and returned with galley proofs of her book. She read from her essay on Thomas.

" 'The black youngsters of today,' I wrote, 'must ask black leaders: If you can't make an effort to reach, reconstruct, and save a black man who has been to and graduated from Yale, how can you reach down here in this drug-filled, hate-filled cesspool where I live and save me?' I went on to say, 'I am supporting Clarence Thomas's nomination, and I am neither naive enough nor hopeful enough to imagine that in publicly supporting him I will give the younger generation a pretty picture of unity, but rather I can show them that I and they come from a people who had the courage to be when being was dangerous, who had the courage to dare when daring was dangerous—and, most important, had the courage to hope. Because Clarence Thomas has been poor, has been nearly suffocated by the acrid odor of racial discrimination, is intelligent, well trained, black, and young enough to be won over again, I support him. The prophet in Lamentations cried, "Although he put his mouth in the dust...there is still hope." ' "

"That's beautifully written, Maya, but it flies in the face of the facts. The facts say that, despite your desire to win him over to the cause of our civil rights and advancement as a people, the brother has gone the other way. And he has no interest in turning back. Hope is a good thing. Hope is a sacred thing. But there is also history. Thomas has a history that has moved in one direction and one direction only. And that's to the extreme right."

"May I quote from your own book?" Maya asked me.

"I'd be flattered."

"In your *Hard Left,* you called the conservatives half right. I liked the phrase. I liked it because you acknowledged that, when it came to their concern for the moral fabric of this country, they had a point. They weren't all wrong. Like them, Tavis, you're half right in your critique of Clarence Thomas. So far there are little signs of a change in his heart. Surely his record for these past five years will justify skepticism. But you're also wrong—and I'd say more than half wrong—in suggesting that any one of us is beyond hope."

"I'd be the last to argue against hope."

"Then don't."

"I won't," I said, smiling. "But only because these butter biscuits have melted my heart and made further argument impossible."

"Good. In discussions such as these, I don't at all mind prevailing. And if my prowess in the kitchen can work in my favor, so much the better!"

I had given it my best shot. I wolfed down a couple more biscuits, gave Mother Maya a big hug, and hurried off to the airport.

A week later, back in Los Angeles, I received a large package from Maya. She sent me a box of flowers—not a traditional bouquet but dozens of loose petals. The sweet fragrance was overwhelming.

"Dear young Tavis Smiley," the inscription read. "Today I want to shower you with petals!"

9

The Art of Listening

I hadn't seen Maya in many months when, much to my delight, she phoned to say she'd be in Los Angeles and wondered whether I might meet her for dinner. She chose Hal's Bar & Grill, a casual but sophisticated restaurant in Venice. We arrived at the same time. Hal, the proprietor and Maya's dear friend, escorted us to a corner table. We sat below a large abstract painting. Maya ordered a drink.

"This place feels like jazz to me," said Maya. "Do you know what I mean?"

"I do," I said. "It has an open vibe."

"That's the spirit of jazz. That's the heart of the black

131

aesthetic. It's hard to think of a black painter, dancer, poet, writer of prose—you name it—who hasn't been deeply influenced by jazz."

"Where do you think that gift for improvisation comes from?" I asked as Maya sipped her sherry and glanced at the menu.

"It's the happy meeting place—the sacred meeting place—where art and survival merge. To survive this country, this hellish American history, we've had to make it up as we go along. We lacked the tools that would otherwise enable us to plan. As a people, there was no way to outline our future. We'd been robbed of our language, robbed of our freedom, robbed of everything save our God-given ability to create art. The art could not be denied because it came through pure spontaneity—the field shout, the blues cry, the musical laments that turned frustration into beauty. You know all this. You know that those shouts and cries and laments could contain a world of feeling. And even though there were times when the songs contained hidden political messages—just as centuries later, the jazz of Max Roach and Abbey Lincoln and Nina Simone contained overt political messages—these musical expressions were essentially prayers. We were asking God for help to see us through. Help came in the very form of the request itself. As a subjugated people struggling to understand our subjugation, we found our voice in the struggle. The act of asking for help became the help. Or to put it another way, the plea became the promise."

Then she said, "I see you're scribbling something on your napkin, Tavis. Are you preparing a rejoinder?"

"No; merely taking notes."

"You won't be quizzed on any of this, I promise," said Maya with a broad smile.

"And you were going to bring it all back to jazz."

As if on cue, a jazz quintet that had assembled in the front of the restaurant broke into song—tenor saxophone, trumpet, piano, bass, and drums. It was as though Hal was providing exactly the kind of music required for Maya to embellish her verbal riffs. She took a few more sips of her sherry before continuing.

"Yes, indeed, it all comes down to jazz," she said. "Early on, the shouts, cries, and laments of our people on the plantations were agricultural art forms. They were about surviving those murderous work fields. Jazz took that same sensibility, modernized it, adapted it, expanded it, and applied it to urban life. New Orleans. Chicago. New York. The murderous cities. How do you keep your head high as you walk the mean streets of Pittsburgh and Detroit? You improvise, dear Tavis. You blow your way through the harsh winters. You cool your way through the steaming summers. You adapt by employing an art form that, in one sense, depends on ultimate relaxation.

"You can never anticipate the beat. If you do, you'll never swing. Swing is dependent on relaxation—on letting the meter move you rather than imposing some rigid meter on your message. Do that and your song will be stiffer than a board. Let God be the timekeeper. You need not worry about time.

"And yet—here's the beautiful paradox—all this relaxation leads to stimulation. Listen to all the fabulous ideas converging in the imagination of Louis Armstrong. Or Miles. Or Monk. Or Sarah Vaughan. Those ideas flow freely because they are born out of relaxation. Louis is cool, Miles is cool, Monk is cool, Sarah is cool because they don't have to anticipate the future. They can deal with the here and now. They can live in the moment. They're in touch with eternity, knowing that eternity is happening with every beat and every breath."

"I'm presuming you once dreamed of being a jazz artist, Maya," I said.

"I gave it a shot. I did all right. I moved from my calypso period to another phase in which I sang jazz numbers. I had gigs at well-known jazz clubs, but when it came to vocal technique, I always knew my limitations. Measured against Ella Fitzgerald or Dinah Washington or Della Reese, I simply couldn't compete. But that doesn't mean I stopped seeing myself as a jazz person. When I acted, when I wrote screenplays, when I directed, when I committed to political activism—all this was done, and continues to be done, as a committed improviser. I move from one activity to another as a horn player moves from chorus to chorus. I suspect you do the same, Tavis."

"Making it up as you go along requires a lot of confidence."

"Every time I see you on that talk show of yours, I see your confidence building. But I do have one critique, if I may."

"Sure. Let me have it."

"Your questions are astute. They show that you're prepared. We have every confidence that you have done your homework. That's good. What isn't quite as good is your ability to listen. I say this to you in love, and I say it plainly. The key to all relationships, whether a private relationship among two friends or a public relationship between an interviewer and interviewee, is listening. Most people feign listening. They do it half-heartedly. They're listening for a pause so that they may break in and speak again. Your eagerness to speak often belies your willingness to listen. I hope I'm not offending you, son."

"I'm listening," I said with a smile. "I'm trying *not* to listen for a pause."

"It's a matter of not simply listening with our ears but listening with our hearts. The heart hears deeply. The heart hears with compassion. And of course the heart— the loving heart—hears with patience. Consequently, when we listen with our hearts we aren't all that anxious to chime in again. It's insecurity that has us asking questions that are overstated and convoluted. It's also insecurity that has us trying to figure out the second question even as our first question is being answered. That takes us out of the moment and makes for stilted jazz. Free-flowing jazz, the kind that feeds our souls, is possible only when we are listening closely and openheartedly to our fellow players. We are nurturing one another. We are in the midst of a miracle of communication that's only possible when we have learned to listen. What do you say, Tavis? Am I rattling on too long?"

"Not at all. Let's order dinner and listen to the jazz; it will give me a little time to absorb the weighty lesson."

"The lesson shouldn't be heavy. It should be light and easy. Like a jazz lick. Like a fetching turn of phrase. The best lessons are the quick ones, the ones that unexpectedly lift the fog and allow us to see the clear light of day."

Our evening at Hal's was long and languorous. Even after dinner and dessert, Maya wanted to linger. I needed no convincing. The more time with Maya, the merrier.

The jazz band had played several spirited sets, and

the late-night mood was mellow. Maya wanted to hear all about my recent trip to Africa, where I interviewed President Bill Clinton, who was especially forthright in discussing our country's historical complicity in the slave trade and our inexcusable inaction against the genocide in Rwanda. I had traveled with Clinton to Botswana, Ghana, Rwanda, Senegal, Uganda, and South Africa.

"You seem to have a rapport with Clinton," said Maya. "He finds favor with you."

"That's an expression my mother would use."

"So would my grandmother. It's an expression close to my heart."

"Because you find favor with everyone."

"Hardly," said Maya. "But it's particularly tricky when the most powerful man in the world finds favor with you. You're so pleased with that favor that you back off from challenging him."

"I noticed that," I said. "Especially someone with Clinton's charm. When he speaks to you, even in a room crowded with world dignitaries, he makes you feel like you're the most important person there."

"And yet I see you were able to push him on some of his policies—the economic policies and drug-sentencing policies discriminating against the poor."

"Could have pushed harder."

"Which would mean no more interviews with him.

Is there any other TV journalist who's been given more one-on-one interviews with Clinton than you?"

At the time it was a dead heat between me and Jim Lehrer at PBS.

"Well, that's a major accomplishment on your part."

By then I knew Maya well enough to realize that at times her praise and encouragement could be overly generous. And yet because she was so sincere, her words never failed to fortify my spirit.

Over at the bar, a couple of well-dressed brothas had been fortifying their spirits with a bit too much booze. On an obviously happy high, they raised their raucous voices high enough to be heard from one side of the restaurant to the other.

"You my *nigger*," said the first. "I mean, my sho'-nuff *nigger!*"

From then on, the N word was furiously bandied about.

Maya was quick to react. She was enraged.

"Let's leave," she said. "I don't to want to hear this."

I suggested a short walk to an outdoor café down the street where we could have a cup of coffee. Maya agreed, and, after settling our bill and saying good night to Hal, we left.

By the time we reached the café, Maya had calmed down.

"I was going to say something to those young men," she said. "I would have if I hadn't been friends with Hal. If they were steady customers, it was not my business to chase them from his establishment. In similar instances, though, I have been known to intervene."

"I believe it."

"I believe it's my duty to point out the toxic nature of that word, no matter who's using it, black or white, man or woman, child or adult. I can't support it. I won't support it."

"I'm afraid, dear Maya, that it's hopeless. The word is here to stay. That train left the station long ago."

"Well, it left without me, dear Tavis, because I'll never accept it. I'll never tolerate it in common usage. It suggests nothing less than the brutal subjugation and degradation of our people. When it is voiced, I can hear our ancestors crying in pain. It prolongs the humiliation they were forced to suffer. I can accept no arguments that justify its use."

"I've never known you, Maya, to reject an argument before hearing one."

"I've heard them all. You're going to tell me that the word has evolved over the years and, in certain contexts, *nigger* no longer means what it once did."

"I do believe that," I said.

"I don't."

"You do believe that the meanings of words change, don't you?" I asked.

"I believe that the word is poison and is contained in a vial marked by a skull and crossbones. If I transfer that poison into a cup of sterling silver or Bavarian crystal, it remains poison. When you consume it, you invite destruction. Just as cyanide can destroy your physical body, certain words can destroy your soul. Either way, poison is poison."

"One's man poison," I said, "can be another man's protein."

"Protein? Tavis, please..."

"For millions of young black men looking to express brotherly solidarity, the word is hardly poisonous."

"You can't change the property of poison," Maya continued to argue. "The poisonous word continues to dehumanize, belittle, and ridicule people."

"But from one generation to another, a word can be turned around to mean its opposite. Take the word *good*. Artists such as James Brown and, later, Michael Jackson used *bad* to mean 'good.' They flipped the script, Maya. They used irony to make their point. They didn't want to adopt the majority culture's linguistic bias. They wanted to undercut the accepted meaning and replace it with its counterpart. Same applies to *nigger*. Rather than accept the middle-class black understanding of the word as being something bad, a new generation turned it into something good. 'My nigger' becomes a term of endearment—bonding together a generation for whom the word's old significance no longer resonates."

"A generation," said Maya, "with a tragically short view of history. A generation with no appreciation of the sacrifices made by their grandmothers and grandfathers."

"But even earlier generations used the word with affection, Maya. I recently read that, on the last day of his life, Dr. King greeted Andrew Young at the Lorraine Motel with the words, 'Li'l nigger, where you been?' That's Dr. King!"

"I can't hear him saying that word. I simply can't. I'd have to question the accuracy of your source."

"But surely you recognize—you must actually know—that good-hearted and sincere black men address one another this way and do so out of love."

"Or out of ignorance. Sorry, Tavis, I will not yield the point. When someone takes his fingernail and scrapes it across a blackboard, the sound is so unnerving that you want to scream. That's the sound I hear when that word falls from the mouths of those who should know better."

"I know better than to push this argument further."

"You recognize the law of diminishing returns."

"I do indeed. Another Maya lesson."

"And a chance to change subjects."

For the rest of the evening, we turned to lighter topics—her induction into the National Women's Hall of Fame as well as the Hollywood movie she had just directed—a first for an African American woman—*Down in the Delta,* with Al Freeman Jr., Esther Rolle, Wesley Snipes, and Alfre Woodard.

It was good to end the evening on a pleasant note.

Back home, though, our N word debate was still rattling around my head. I knew I had been unable to make a dent in the armor of Maya's ironclad argument. For all her progressive thinking, on this one issue I saw her as out of touch with the changing times.

And then, when I turned on the television to lull myself to sleep, an amazing coincidence:

There was a rerun of a Richard Pryor television special that had originally aired in 1977. Celebrated as a towering comedic genius, Pryor made liberal use of the N word—it was one of his trademarks. In fact, he titled his 1974 Grammy Award–winning album *That Nigger's Crazy.* Even those comics who eschewed the word, including Bill Cosby, recognized the essential and effective role it played in Pryor's self-styled lexicon.

I loved Pryor. I saw beyond his ability to crack me up; he was more than a comic to me. He was a great actor, a great creator of brilliant scenarios. He courageously revealed his vulnerabilities—his deepest fears and secret anxieties—with startling candor. He was an original.

I hadn't seen this show before. When it was first broadcast I was thirteen, and in my parents' household such programs were strictly forbidden. So on this night, alone at home, I couldn't wait to watch it.

It was wonderful. It was prime-time Pryor. But what took my breath away—what absolutely floored me—was a long dramatic skit he performed with Dr. Maya Angelou!

It begins in a bar, where the bartender, a young John Belushi, puts Pryor, playing a wino named Willie, out on the street. It's closing time. Willie has no choice but to go home and face his wife. "Please, God," he says, "don't let me be sick. Get me through this one and I'll get through the next one myself." At this point, the scene is drained of all humor. This is serious stuff.

Willie makes it home, where his wife, played by Maya, is waiting for him. The second he arrives, he passes out on the couch. For the rest of the skit, Maya, wearing a pink terry-cloth robe, delivers a monologue that relays her history with Willie—how his drinking has led to his ruination. Her voice drenched in sarcasm, she says, "I get to talk to you intimately like this every night. And I get to see you in the morning—sick, tired, and disgusted." She describes her encounter with a social worker who had asked why in the world she stays with

Willie. "How can I explain to her that I see you like you were on our first date? You were so sassy. Your shoulders used to ride high, like the breasts of young girls. And you used to call me things like I was something good to eat—honey, baby, sweetie." She goes on to describe how a disastrous economy wore him down, and he lost job after job. "I used to watch you go to the welcome table," she said, "and come back with dry bones."

With tears in her eyes, Maya says, "And then you called yourself a nigger. And I said, 'Honey, oh, don't call yourself that.' And you said, 'Oh, no, it's an affectionate term. I can use it, but no one else can use it.' And then you called me a nigger, Willie. And if there was ever any affection in it, it disappeared. Because you started using it to curse me, to curse yourself, to curse the whole race. To curse life, Willie. And then the booze. The booze began to take my place. It was closer than a friend and truer than a wife."

Seated in a chair across from Willie, Maya lets all her pent-up feeling flow freely. "I hate you!" she cries. "I hate you until you come home." With those words spoken, she gets up and goes over to her husband. "But when you come home, I love you, Willie." Now she is moaning, like a blues singer, a jazz singer. Now she is saying, "I know you're not what you wanted to be, Willie, and you're not what I wanted you to be, but I'm yours, Willie, and you're mine, and when I forget that, there ain't nothing else worth remembering."

I was stunned.

The next day I called Maya at her hotel. She was just about to check out. I told her about watching the rerun of the Pryor show.

"I didn't realize it was on," she said.

"It was beautiful," I said. "You were magnificent. What a performance!"

"Well, thank you, son. It felt good doing it. And talk about jazz—I do believe I improvised that entire scene. There was no script."

"So you wrote it," I said.

"At the moment of execution—yes."

"And in it, your character was able to show Pryor, the world's biggest proponent of the N word, the error of his ways."

"It just came out of me, naturally."

"What was Pryor's reaction? What did he say to you after the skit?"

"Oh, he was highly complimentary. He loved it."

"And yet..."

"He kept on using the word until a few years later, when he went to Africa. You remember his famous comment when he returned from the Motherland, don't you?"

"I do. He said he didn't see any niggers in Africa. Only beautiful black people. And he promised not to use the word again."

"That was nearly twenty years ago. I'm not sure he kept that promise. But I am sure that he is one of our most profound artists. I remember when he was first coming up in Greenwich Village and was due to open for Miles Davis. Miles turned the tables and insisted that he—Miles—open for Richard. Coming from Miles, with his strong sense of self, that was a notable act of humility—one great jazz artist acknowledging another."

"Have you stayed in touch with Pryor over the years?" I asked.

"Off and on. I'm afraid that scene proved prophetic. Richard really has turned into Willie."

"I want to watch it again."

"I think they sent me a copy of the show. During your next trip to North Carolina, we'll watch it together. I'm glad you liked it, though. And I'm glad you've swung over to my side about avoiding that poisonous word at all costs."

I laughed and said, "I wouldn't go that far."

"I would go even further. I would say one day you'll see that not only that one word but also all vulgarity is injurious to your heart and the hearts of others."

"I know that's right."

"And know one other thing, Tavis. Cherishing language—especially the language we speak—requires courage."

"That word again."

"I can't get away from it. The truth is that it takes courage to forge and maintain a language free of vulgarity. We naturally yearn for the acceptance of our peers. We're tempted to trade in the lingua franca that purportedly bonds us to our brothers and sisters. We don't want to miss out on what we perceive as camaraderie. And, yes, camaraderie, especially among our peers, is a sweet thing. So to step outside of that linguistic universe and stand alone is an act of bravery."

"Or an act of love," I added. "Love of language."

"So we're back to our old argument."

"Not an argument," I said. "A loving study in differences."

"A courageous study," Maya added with what I imagined, over that long telephone wire, was a wide smile and quick wink.

10

Grace and Disgrace

It wasn't many months after my long dinner with Maya in Venice that I found myself facing a major moment in my career: President Clinton had agreed to let me conduct the first one-on-one interview with him since the Monica Lewinsky scandal erupted.

I was excited and even flattered, but I could hardly take credit. For Clinton, I just happened to be the right person at the right time. The interview was happening on the Monday before the Tuesday midterm elections. Impeachment hearings were only two days off. The president desperately needed to pick up congressional seats—members who would vote against the articles of impeachment. He had no choice but to galvanize his black base. Appearing on BET would go a long way toward achieving that end.

The night before the encounter, I had a lot on my mind. The interview, a major exclusive, was certain to attract a huge audience. I wanted to be fair, but I also didn't want to neglect the urgency of the issue: Had the president been lying? Though I never adopted the "I got you" attitude of many reporters and was not, in fact, out to get Clinton, I certainly didn't want to be used by him.

With all these thoughts swirling around in my head, I decided to call Mother Maya. Who better to help me through the maze of my feelings?

"It's a beautiful opportunity, son," she said when I explained what I was about to do. "A beautiful blessing. But also a grave responsibility."

"How aggressive do you think I should be?" I asked.

"I wouldn't say *aggressive*. I'd say *assertive*. Aggression feels like an invasion. Warriors are aggressive. I know you well enough, Tavis, to know that you are not interested in invading his private life. Were it not for the fact that there were pending articles of impeachment, you wouldn't be having this conversation at all. But those articles give you every right to assert yourself."

"It's a matter of tone," I said.

"Our tone reflects the conditions of our hearts. If

our hearts are bitter, our tone is sarcastic. If our hearts are closed, our tone is pinched. If our hearts are angry, our tone is belligerent. In addressing the president of the United States—and you have done this many times by now, Tavis—your tone has always been respectful. That's your only concern. The man may answer your question forthrightly, or he may, as I suspect he will, employ subterfuge. Either way, I envision you remaining steady, pressing him when appropriate, and backing off when you know you've gone as far as you can go."

"Knowing that is really the key, isn't it?"

"It's just another occasion when our favorite formula—the law of diminishing returns—allows us to see the futility of pressing on."

"I don't want to be seen as a patsy."

"It's good to vent that fear, Tavis. It's good to vent all fears. Fears need to be given voice so that they don't overwhelm our minds. But, sweetheart, that's one fear you don't have to worry about. You are not a patsy. You will have prepared thoughtful and thorough questions for the man. You will give him a run for his money. And that's all you can do. Be yourself, and you'll be the man God intended you to be."

"I usually don't suffer performance anxiety," I said, as if to apologize for leaning on Maya for support.

"I don't, either. But that doesn't mean that I wasn't

nervous as hell before certain performances. Speaking of our dear President Clinton, before I read 'On the Pulse of Morning' on that cold January day, I was shivering with frail nerves."

"I would not have guessed it. You looked cool as a cucumber."

"My external calm belied an interior terror. After all, I was facing a worldwide audience. Would my voice crack? Would my verse hold up? Would my cadence falter and my audience start to snooze?"

I had to laugh. "Oh, come on—when has a Maya Angelou audience ever snoozed?"

"When you perform avant-garde theater—as I did, in Genet's *The Blacks* in Greenwich Village—you will inevitably find yourself facing a few snoozers. But when you face the president tomorrow and deftly probe into his private melodrama, which has turned into political theater, no one will be snoozing, I can assure you."

"Any last words of wisdom?"

"Only to be aware of his beguiling charm. By the way, if the president were to call me tonight for advice about handling you—and I strongly suspect he will not—I'd tell dear Bill the same thing—'Beware of Tavis's beguiling charm!'"

"Thanks for charming me into a restful sleep."

"Sweet dreams, son."

I was, in fact, able to fall asleep easily. I awoke refreshed and ready to go. As usual, Maya had combined practicality with spirituality. Her practical advice—be assertive, not aggressive. Her spiritual advice—be yourself.

During the interview, I was myself. And Clinton was Clinton. I might well have achieved a well-balanced, assertive tone, but it hardly mattered. He was evasive to a fault. No matter how deft my line of questioning, he found a way to avoid giving clear answers. Early on, I saw that the more I pursued, the more he displayed his skill at circumvention. In the end, I don't believe I did myself harm. I conducted a responsible interview. But I was able to elicit no new responses or create any headlines. Clearly, his beguiling charm trumped mine.

Some months later Maya called after watching an interview I had done with Fidel Castro in Havana. She was curious about the encounter. I told her that in the middle of the night I'd been called to the presidential palace, where, through a translator, I talked to Castro until dawn. I told her a funny story about what happened when I asked him to autograph a photography book about Cuba. Castro looked it over and declared that a book like that belongs in Havana, not Los Angeles, and he insisted on keeping it for himself.

Maya howled. "Oh, dear Lord! The dictator was about to steal your precious souvenir. What in the world was young Tavis Smiley going to do? Take on Castro and wind up in some cold jail cell or assert his rights as an American citizen?"

"I gently suggested that, as an appreciator of Cuban culture, I treasured the memories of this wonderful trip and would always hold the book dear to my heart."

"And what did our Mr. Castro have to say about that?"

"He said, 'Give me the book. It's staying in Cuba.'"

"To which you replied..."

"Wish I could, Mr. President, but it's my only copy, and I couldn't deprive my friends and family the opportunity to view your glorious country through these priceless photographs."

"You held your ground, Tavis!"

"Barely."

"And got to keep the book?"

"Barely. He gave me one last devilish look to see whether I would concede. But I held the book tightly in my hand. He finally relented."

"And he autographed the thing?"

"He did, Maya. Next time you're in town, I'll show you."

"Proud of you, son. You stood up to the man."

"In a very minor and meaningless confrontation," I said.

"Do not demean yourself. A lesser soul would have folded like a house of cards."

"We'll see if I'm ever invited back to the presidential palace."

"When you are, you'll take me with you. Meanwhile, onward and upward. I'm proud of your progress."

And then the progress stopped.

I was in my fifth year at BET. Although I was grateful for the exposure that network had given me, BET was notorious for its lack of organization and planning. In the media world, this was hardly a secret. When in an interview with *Newsweek* I mentioned that the network faced challenges, BET boss Bob Johnson cussed me out during a speakerphone call in front of his staff. I argued back, saying that this was the first time I had heard from Johnson in four years. Never once had I received even a simple note after doing interviews with everyone from the president to the pope. That was our first rough run-in. In our second, he unceremoniously fired me. Here's how it happened:

My deal with BET allowed my own production company to sell news stories that I thought might be attractive to other networks. When I managed to secure an exclusive interview with Sara Jane Olson, the Symbionese Liberation Army fugitive who'd been caught after twenty-three years on the run, I didn't see it as a

BET story. Ms. Olson was a white soccer mom. I offered the story to *60 Minutes* because the show's network, CBS, was owned by the same conglomerate that owned BET, Viacom. *60 Minutes* passed because Dan Rather had been chasing the same story. So I sold it to ABC's *Primetime Thursday.* When it aired, the ratings were sensational, and it beat the pants off CBS's show during the same time slot, a new version of *Dragnet.*

Viacom skewered Johnson for letting one of his underlings—me—sell the competition a news segment that hurt CBS. Johnson failed to explain that not only was I within my contractual rights but also that my story had been rejected by CBS. In a public way, Johnson canned me. It became a national story. I had strong support—so strong, in fact, that Johnson had to take to the air to defend my firing. But he never wavered. He painted me as disloyal, unappreciative, and self-serving.

The humiliation was devastating.

I had gone from being the highest-paid broadcaster—and most visible newsman and political advocate—in the history of BET to its most famous discard. The ride to the top took five years. But the fall to the bottom took only a minute. When Johnson said, "Smiley is out," I had no recourse. I was gone.

I sulked. I sank. I retreated. For days my phone rang off the wall, but I didn't really want to talk. I didn't have any comments for the press. I didn't have much to say to my friends. I really just wanted to run and hide. But before I did, one friend made sure I didn't.

It was Maya calling from North Carolina.

"Have you sent him a thank you note?" she asked.

"Sent who what?"

"You heard me, son. Have you sent him a thank you note?"

"Maya," I said, "whom are you talking about?"

"The man who's most on your mind."

"Bob Johnson?"

"Who else? Forgive me for repeating myself, but I must ask you again. Have you sent him a thank you note?"

"I have not."

"Then get busy, son. I'd strongly suggest you call off the pity party and send that gentleman a note of gratitude."

"For unceremoniously firing me?"

"Yes, and for opening up your life as it has never been opened before. I see this as a grand day, Tavis. I truly do. A grand opportunity to step out and move on. You're starting a fabulous new chapter in your life. And were it not for dear Mr. Johnson, that chapter would be postponed. Now it is most imminent."

I was speechless. Maya was so cheerful, so absolutely ebullient, that I couldn't possibly return to despair.

"And when you've written the thank you note," she

added, "then I suggest getting on your knees and praying for his good health and continued prosperity."

"I'm not sure that—"

"I am. I am sure that the only way of dealing with negative energy is to turn it on its ear. You do that by redirecting that energy. You acknowledge the hidden blessing. You also do that by recognizing that whatever happened has happened for a reason. You don't need to know the reason now. In fact, looking to decipher the reason will only lead to frustration. Only faith can defeat frustration. And only prayer—powerful, positive prayer directed at those whom you believe have harmed you—can turn you around."

Right then and there, without any prompting on my part, my dear friend Maya broke into song. Her voice was strong, sweet, and filled with joy:

When God shut Noah in the grand old ark
He put a rainbow in the cloud
When thunders rolled and the sky was dark
God put in a rainbow in the cloud...

Away down yonder in Egypt's sand
God put in a rainbow in the cloud
Just to lead his children to the promised land
God put in a rainbow in the cloud...

When they put old Daniel in the lion's den
God put a rainbow in the cloud
Just to prove his promise to the sons of men
God put a rainbow in the cloud.

When the song was over, I tried holding back tears but failed. I wept like a child and began putting pen to paper.

PART THREE

Courage

II

Breath

I was shocked. Maya was on a respirator. For the first time since I had known her, she looked frail and vulnerable. I couldn't help but be concerned. I tried to hide my feelings but quickly found out that's an impossible feat in Maya's presence.

"I'm fine, sweetheart," she said. "Just need a little extra oxygen now and then. Welcome to Harlem."

It was 2005, and I had come to visit her in the four-story brownstone she had bought on 120th Street. Although Maya needed round-the-clock help, she was still reading voraciously and still writing every day.

Reading and writing were like breathing for her. I noticed a large magnifying glass on the table.

For the past few months she had spoken about the inordinate amount of work she had put into her building's restoration.

"This old house," she said, "was something like me. It might have been broken down, but its soul was intact. I just needed to restore that soul. Because I was blessed and highly favored, I was able to do just that."

The house was magnificent—a first-floor front parlor, a formal dining room, five bedrooms, three full bathrooms—with all sorts of interesting nooks and crannies. There was an ornate stairway leading to the upper floors, but Maya had installed an elevator. Moving around had become difficult. She walked steadily, but with great caution and the help of a cane.

As I remarked on the charm of her home, I continued to repress my alarm over Maya's physical condition. Her mental condition, however, seemed not in the least impaired. As always, she was filled with spirit.

She showed me her splendid master bedroom, adorned with heavy burgundy brocade draperies, and the guest bedrooms, where her son, Guy, and his family would be staying over the upcoming holidays.

Back downstairs, we settled into a sunlit yellow

breakfast nook situated at the back of the house. We sat together and held hands, as we often did.

"This is the coziest spot," she said. "The spot most conducive to talking."

The initial talk centered on her remarkable domestic do-over.

"How did you find this wonderful place?" I asked her.

"I didn't," she said. "Nick Ashford and Val Simpson found it for me. It's a landmark property first built in 1881. When they discovered it was for sale, they called me and described it over the phone. They said it was in a state of ruination but had fabulous potential. I trust Nick and Val implicitly. I trust all my friends implicitly. I bought it sight unseen. When I finally did come up from North Carolina to see it, I was shocked—a little like the shock you experienced when you saw me today, Tavis."

"I wouldn't say I was shocked—"

"Come, come, Tavis. You didn't know that I require extra oxygen these days. Well, this old house—which had been vandalized time and time again—required an extravagant amount of work to get it up and running. Now that the work is done, I can say with some pride that this noble edifice has been brought back to its original glory—and then some! For a lady in her late seventies to take on this task might seem unadvisable. But to rebuild and revitalize a crumbling edifice was exactly the kind of project required to rebuild and revitalize my life. It gave me purpose."

"As though you lacked purpose before," I said. "You're still writing. I see your new book everywhere."

For the previous few minutes, Maya had been speaking without the use of her respirator. But then she had to insert the tubes in her nose to facilitate her breathing.

"This struggle to breathe is profound," she said, speaking in a slow and measured cadence. The rich, mellifluous tone was still there, but not the easy flow. She had to stop between words and modulate the force with which she spoke. "The need for oxygen has me remembering that earlier part of my life when I went mute. I chose not to use words because I saw my words as instruments of harm. Once I saw the light—that words can be instruments of healing—you couldn't shut me up. From then on, I'm afraid I took for granted that even stream of breath over which our words flow. I couldn't imagine my words not flowing. Now that the flow has been compromised, I find that I must choose my words even more carefully, Tavis. Words have become that much more precious. If I once assumed that the great reservoir of language was an infinite phenomenon, today I must realize its finite nature. I only have so many words left."

"And yet I hear you say that, Maya, with no fear."

"None whatsoever. Decades ago I gave death its due. I looked at it unflinchingly. I even spoke to it. I said, 'You win. I will never overcome you. But what I can overcome is the dread you provoke. Once I truly accept your inevitability, I can breathe'—there's that word again, Tavis—'yes, I can breathe a sigh of relief. I no longer have to try to defeat you. Your domain is permanent. But it lives in the future.

"'It is not here today. Today I am alive, and as long as I am alive I will act lively. I will celebrate the blood coursing through my veins. I will celebrate my ability to put one foot in front of the other. I will celebrate the unseen, mysterious, but altogether loving God who has given me this life. You, Mr. Death, will not interfere with that celebration. I simply won't allow it. So go on and see after your domain. I'm not there yet.' And until I get there, I'm going to keep singing the song my grandmother sang back in Stamps, Arkansas:

I've got shoes, you've got shoes
All of God's children got shoes
When I get to heaven gonna put on my shoes
Gonna walk all over God's heaven

I've got a harp, you've got a harp
All of God's children got a harp

When I get to heaven gonna play on my harp
Gonna play all over God's heaven

I've got a song, you've got a song
All God's children got a song
When I get to heaven gonna sing a new song
Gonna sing all over God's heaven."

Maya didn't sing quite as loudly or robustly as before, but her voice was sweet as ever. Her voice was filled with conviction.

"This respirator is certainly a nuisance," she admitted, "and nothing I had wished for. Like most people, I am vain, and this machine does nothing to enhance my public presentation. But if it gives me new breath, as it surely does, then I have no choice but to view it as a blessing."

Maya knew about blessings, and the blessing that she had earlier identified in my life—my forced departure from BET—had by then manifested itself ten times over.

I had found high-profile work with ABC, CNN, and National Public Radio. NPR proved an especially good fit for me because I was given the freedom to address complex and controversial subjects. Then five days a week, *The Tavis Smiley Show* tackled the tough issues and, in doing so, showcased dozens of major political and cultural figures.

Maya was among my first guests. She came on to celebrate Thanksgiving. It was 2002, the year she turned seventy-four. Before the interview began, she spoke about new health concerns. I didn't detect apprehension on her part. She was merely reporting her news.

"Increasingly," she said, "the aging process has become central to my story. I can't avoid it. I won't avoid it. It brings to mind an old adage often quoted by my blues friends, like B. B. King: 'I've paid the dues to tell the news.' The longer you live, the keener your obligation to report on the journey. I see it as a chance to comfort those coming up behind me. I'm saying, 'I'm here. The water's fine. Jump on in.'"

When we got on the air, I asked Maya about the challenge of maintaining a grateful demeanor in the face of ever-increasing health problems.

"Each day I am more grateful," she replied. "It is said that courage doesn't come from bravado. Nor does it come from being brave in easy times. It comes from being brave in dangerous times. Being grateful is best enjoyed when one's very life is threatened—when the devil is afoot and terrorism is nigh, when young men call black women bitches and hos.

"During this time, when the African American is still

belittled, even in the mouths of many liberated whites, it is imperative to be grateful. Be grateful for your very life, be grateful for your ability to strengthen and rebuild your self-worth, grateful for one more chance to the fight the good fight and walk the good walk, grateful for one more day to show someone some kindness and courtesy, grateful for one more moment to show somebody some love."

Maya had told me she had no reservations about discussing her health. Thus my next question:

"Because you are such a grateful person, Dr. Angelou, what has gone through your mind over the last few days, given that your sight is now being compromised?"

"More gratitude, Tavis. There's always room for more. I'm grateful for my doctor, grateful that I have the means to pay him for his expertise, grateful for the technology that allows him to understand my ocular condition. The deterioration of my ocular condition, however, need not injure my spiritual condition. My spiritual condition is strong. That condition has me speaking out against cruelty, against the disenfranchisement of anybody, male or female, gay or straight, black or white, Asian, Arab, or Jew.

"On these matters I do not hedge. I do not wait for opportunity. As soon as the issue informs my consciousness, I do whatever I can do. That allows me to look in the mirror each morning when I brush my teeth and not feel ashamed.

"The deterioration of our bodies does not excuse the deterioration of our resolve. Our bodies are mere vessels that contain our spirits. Our spirits are eternal. Our spirits reflect not only our ancestors, who have informed and galvanized our hearts, but they also reflect the living God of love. That love lives outside of time. It is endless. Injury, incapacitation, even death—nothing impedes the flow of love. That flow refreshes. It is that same beautiful onrushing flow that keeps us young, even as we grow old."

When the interview was over, it was clear to me that I had far more concern about Maya's physical problems than she did. Whereas the notion of her mortality alarmed me—I couldn't envision a world without Maya Angelou—she viewed the prospect with serenity. She did more than accept the inevitable; she used her physical challenges as further motivation to keep working, writing, traveling, performing, and playing her part on the public stage, her essential part.

12

The Good Word

I lost it.

I lost my temper and, in doing so, lost all verbal restraint. One of my employees, a producer, had made a major mistake. As a result, several of my broadcasts had been improperly edited. I thought the result reflected poorly on my professionalism—and I flipped out. I called the woman, who was also a good friend, into the studio and read her the riot act. I cursed a blue streak.

Cursing came to me relatively late in life—in college. Before then, my church training held. I never employed vulgarity. But when the wide world opened up to me at Indiana University, my lexicon expanded to include the street slang of the athletes who were my dorm mates. I used that language sparingly, but when I discovered my producer's power of oversight, I used that language excessively.

The producer simply sat there and endured the tongue-lashing. She knew me well enough to know that my fury would soon pass. It did. We were cool. I regained my composure and presumed that was the end of that. In fact, that was just the beginning.

A sound engineer had taped my entire tirade and saw fit to send it to the top brass at NPR. They were alarmed. They demanded that I sign a new contract, complete with a behavior clause that forbade any outbreak of this kind. I was embarrassed and humiliated and had no choice but to sign it.

In the middle of all this, I had scheduled an interview with Maya, who was on the road promoting a cookbook. She was coming to my headquarters on Crenshaw Boulevard, in the heart of Los Angeles's black arts district. I had purchased a building that held my offices and studio.

"I want to see the fruits of your labor," she told me. "A proud mother always celebrates the success of her children."

Her arrival caused great excitement. She wore a long skirt, a brilliantly colored blouse, and an African-print head wrap. She was radiant. It hardly mattered that she moved with difficulty or that her breathing was labored and her eyesight compromised. Her great dignity remained intact. Her spirit soared that afternoon. Graciously, she stopped and spoke with everyone, allowing pictures to be taken, passing out praise, and generating goodwill at every turn.

During her interview she spoke of her book *Hallelujah! The Welcome Table: A Lifetime of Memories with Recipes* with the eager excitement of a first-time author. She told an endearing story about the time when she was still in her mute period in Stamps, Arkansas, and a teacher had slapped her for not speaking. When Maya's grandmother found out, she came to school and confronted the teacher.

"Are you somebody's grandbaby?" she asked the teacher.

"I am somebody's grandbaby," the teacher replied.

"Well, this child here is my grandbaby," said Maya's grandmother before slapping the teacher across her face.

Later Maya was told by her grandmother, "Nobody has the right to hit nobody in the face, but I was just trying to teach you a lesson."

That night her grandmother presented her with a sumptuous caramel cake, the recipe for which is included in the cookbook.

"And the lesson learned?" I asked Maya.

"That I was loved. That I was protected. And that my grandmother went against her own principles to show me how she valued me and respected my right to stay silent."

"And the icing on the cake..."

"Was the cake itself!" Maya exclaimed.

We both laughed. Afterward, we continued the conversation in my office.

"I'm glad you told that story about your grandmother on the air," I said.

"To tell you the truth, Tavis, for a long time I blamed myself for what happened. I felt that my inability to talk had caused the confrontation. In my little-girl mind, I said to myself, 'You talk too much or you don't talk at all. But either way, you wind up hurting somebody.' It took me years to sort out those feelings. When to speak up and when to stay silent—that's always a challenge. In your case, though, I've seen that you've achieved a most felicitous balance between speaking and listening."

"I wish. You're the most generous listener I've ever encountered, Maya. You're the gold standard for listening. I wish I hadn't abandoned that standard the other day."

"What in the world happened the other day?" asked Maya.

"I went off."

"Tell me about it, son."

As I told the whole sordid tale, Maya listened with rapt attention. When I was through, her only comment was "Oh." It was a soft "oh," an empathetic "oh," an "oh" that indicated that she had absorbed the turmoil I was experiencing.

"Would you mind if I told you a little story?" she asked.

"Make it a long story," I said.

"There's not much to it. It happened decades ago. I was living in San Francisco, a single mother raising my young son. San Francisco was really my mother's city, not mine. It was there that she owned pool halls and gambling clubs and lived in a large Victorian house on Fulton Street, where she had her own cook. She dressed beautifully and was well respected as a successful businesswoman. She was willing to help me in any way she could. But my self-esteem required that I remain independent of her. For the most part I was. My son and I lived in two small rented rooms. I worked two jobs at once, the first as a fry cook in a diner. I had to be there every morning at five. The second job was as a cook in a Creole restaurant, from four in the afternoon to nine at night. Somewhere along the line I worked in a record store in the Fillmore District, hawking the latest bebop and rhythm and blues. All this is to say that I was among the people. I cooked food that nourished their souls and sold music that lifted their spirits. I spoke their salty language. That was the language of the streets. One friend even called me a poet of profanity.

"Then one day my mother startled me by saying, 'Baby, I just have to say that I see you as one of the great women of the world. I really do. I put you on the same plateau as Eleanor Roosevelt and Dr. Mary McLeod Bethune. You exhibit kindness to everyone you meet. You're intelligent, you're sweet, you speak beautifully, and you're overflowing with love. I must give you a kiss this very moment.'

"She kissed me on the lips and then suddenly changed subjects. I was astounded. I was close to tears. Her praise came out of nowhere, but it was so earnest, so powerfully sincere, that I found myself thinking about what she had said for days afterward. Keep in mind that at this point I had not made a name for myself. It was hard to accept my mother's celebration of me. At the same time, I knew that my mother was not given to mindless compliments. What if she was right? Could I actually be capable of greatness? And if so, how should I comport myself? It was right then and there that I decided to take my mother's words to heart. I decided to speak as though everything my mother said was true. At that moment

profanity lost its appeal. I would certainly not judge anyone else who cursed. Nor would I use language to try to
sound superior or condescending. It was more a matter
of realizing my higher self—the self that my mother recognized with such clarity.

"It turned out to be easier than I thought, Tavis.
Whenever heightened emotions came over me, I avoided
the old default position. I found other ways—more de-
scriptive ways—to express myself. Of course there were
times when I slipped. Occasionally I still do. When it
happens, I don't scold myself. I see it merely as a
reminder to be more conscious. As I went on with my life
and found myself in the public eye, my decision turned
out to be a blessing. In terms of language, it has forced
me to be far more creative."

"I hear you, Maya," I said.

"You are much further along than I was when I made
the decision to clean up my act. In that regard, I think it's
vital that you see this episode as a dire warning. As public people, we're terribly vulnerable. Some people may
view us as heroic today, but others are eager to portray
us as villains tomorrow. They're looking for excuses to
do just that. To give them an excuse—to give them the
rope with which to hang us—is really an exercise in self-
destruction. All this is to say that your tantrum—if I
might call it that—"

"That's what it was."

"Your tantrum will turn out to be another one of those blessings in disguise. Now that you've done it once and seen its ugly consequences, I trust you have the foresight never to do it again. Besides, a decision to elevate one's language is a decision to draw one closer to God."

"In what sense?" I asked.

"In the sense that we thank Him for our gift of speech by turning our speech into an ongoing prayer of praise. I think of that gift when I sing

I heard the voice of Jesus say,
'I am this dark world's light;
Look unto Me, thy morn shall rise,
And all thy day be bright.'
I looked to Jesus, and I found
In Him my star, my sun;
And in that light of life I'll walk
Till traveling days are done."

I sang along with Maya, knowing that, from that day forward, my vocabulary would never be what it once was.

Not to say it still couldn't expand. "It's a great vocabulary test," Maya assured me. "I'm certain you'll be great at it."

"What's it called?"

"Word Crunch."

I was at her home in Winston-Salem, making one of my periodic visits. We were seated in the kitchen, always her favorite spot, and we had chatted amiably about how good I felt about purging myself of profane language.

"When those stale old go-to words are finally discarded," she said, "it's amazing how our language is enriched. It's as though for your entire life you've restricted yourself to peanut butter sandwiches and suddenly someone introduces you to deep-dish black-iron pot roast. In fact, if you can beat me at Word Crunch, Tavis, your prize is an extra portion of that very special pot roast that I'm cooking us for dinner."

"That's all the motivation I need," I said. "Let's get cracking."

At a game whose object is to take a dozen scrambled letters and make as many words as you can, I didn't have a prayer against Maya. If I constructed a dozen words, in no time flat Maya doubled that. She found words within words—short, pithy words; long, archaic words—simple words, witty words, words that had my head spinning. It was a little like playing a game of singles against Serena Williams.

"You did yourself proud," said Maya after defeating me in nine out of ten games.

"I'm not sure you didn't let me win that last one," I said.

"Never! You require no sympathy. I would have gladly shut you out, dear Tavis, but you rallied like a champ."

Of course it was Maya who was rallying her spirit against an onslaught of health concerns. The rally was something to be behold. Her mobility, vision, and breathing were all markedly challenged. She moved much more slowly, she saw less, and was dependent on her respirator. Yet as ever, she seemed an endless source of energy. Her curiosity was just as keen and her humor just as sharp. She was just as eager to extend her supportive friendship to others and remain an active presence on the stage of literature and popular culture.

When she traveled, she did so in a custom-fitted bus. When she lectured, she managed without a respirator. She was able to shore up enough oxygen before beginning to speak. She wore dark glasses to protect her eyes.

"Some say I wear sunglasses to try to look hip," she joked, "but I contend that I was born hip. I was born cool. I need no adornments to prove my coolness. My shades are, as W. C. Fields said about his drinking, 'strictly for medicinal purposes.'"

She spoke about a new book she was planning to release for her eightieth birthday, *Letter to My Daughter*. She read me a portion of the introduction to the collection of essays that said, "I gave birth to one child, a son, but I have thousands of daughters. You are black and white, Jewish and Muslim, Asian, Spanish-speaking, Native American, and Aleut. You are fat and thin and pretty and plain, gay and straight, educated and unlettered, and I am speaking to you all."

That evening, after the pot roast—and yes, I was offered an extra portion in spite of my crushing Word Crunch defeats—and after the crackling corn bread, the seasoned collard greens, and the mouthwatering lemon meringue pie, she asked whether I had seen Tyler Perry's recent film *Madea's Family Reunion.*

"I did," I said, "but only because I knew you were in it. As your loyal fan, I couldn't stay away."

"I take it you're not a Tyler Perry fan."

"I admire his marketing genius. But to be honest, Maya, I'm surprised that you took the role in a Madea film."

"Because…" Maya egged me on.

"Because, at least in my mind, Madea stands out as a superficial and even demeaning caricature of strong black women. I would have thought you, of all people, would see her as an insult."

"I see her as a joke."

I sensed that Maya was, as usual, open to hearing a

dissenting point of view, and so for the next few minutes we went at it.

"You're a serious writer, Mother Maya, a serious actor—"

"So are Cicely Tyson, Lynn Whitfield, and Blair Underwood, who appeared in the movie with me."

"Their decision is understandable," I said. "They make their living as actors. They need exposure. But that's hardly the case with you."

"And if I told you, dear Tavis, that I did it because I thought it would be fun, what would you say?"

"I'd say that I still have doubts about the central character of Madea. You don't think she perpetuates a dangerous stereotype?"

"No more so than Flip Wilson's Geraldine."

"That was decades ago, Maya. Geraldine was sassy *and* smart. Besides, we've made progress since then. Madea isn't simply vulgar, she's willful and manipulative, a matriarch who has to control everyone and everything around her. Does that honor the image of the black mother or black grandmother?"

"What I would call low comedy, Tavis, must be measured by a different standard than highbrow theatrical wit. Tyler Perry is hardly August Wilson, nor does he try to be. What he has done, though, is to create an entertainment empire that has given employment to thousands of blacks and provided entertainment that millions of blacks find satisfying."

"But are you, Maya, among those millions who find his brand of humor satisfying?"

"Underneath it all, I applaud his values. His heart is in the right place."

"And that makes him immune," I said, "to the kind of intelligent critique you would normally apply to a film or play?"

"He hired me as an actor, not a critic."

"Am I wrong to say that his humor—especially Madea, his signature creation—panders to the public taste?"

"I can't argue taste," said Maya.

"But is it *your* taste?"

"It's certainly the taste of millions of moviegoers, Tavis."

"So is much of the rap music that you term misogynistic. Millions love it, but that doesn't stop you from condemning it. This is the first time I've ever heard you use popularity to justify art."

"Are we talking about art, Tavis, or are we talking about entertainment?"

"I'm not sure the distinction matters."

"Oh, but it matters a great deal. The purpose of art is to pierce the veil and reveal a deeper reality than the one we normally perceive. Art strives to awaken the mind and stir the soul. Entertainment has a less weighty function. Entertainment is light fare. It's about diversion. Rather than deepen reality, entertainment helps us escape it. It helps us take ourselves less seriously."

"Are you saying that I take myself too seriously?"

"Of course you do, Tavis. That's part of your charm. I wouldn't want you to be any other way."

She was sharp as a tack. "Now it's your charm, Maya, that's derailing our discussion!"

"To the contrary. I find our discussion scintillating. It makes me want to reach out to Mr. Tyler Perry to see if he has another role for me in one of his movies. I need the exposure!"

I had to laugh.

"Well, his movie certainly gave you exposure."

"Not just me, but my poetry. In *Madea's Family Reunion* Tyler had me read a poem that, as a result of being included in that film, got more exposure than anything I have ever written."

I had no counterargument, only a request.

"Would you mind reading it to me now?"

"I'd love to. I call it 'In and Out of Time.'"

Though her glasses were shaded, I could still see Maya close her eyes, and, in the calmest and most musical of voices, she recited her verse:

The Good Word

The sun has come
the mists have gone
we see in the distance
our long way home

I was always yours to have
you were always mine
we have loved each other
in and out of time

When the first stone looked up at the blazing sun
and the first tree struggled up from the forest floor
I have always loved you more

You freed your braids
gave your hair to the breeze
it hung like a hive of honey bees

I reached in the mass
for the sweet honeycomb there
Hah
God how I loved your hair

You saw me bludgeoned by circumstance
lost, injured, hurt by chance

I screamed to the Heavens
loudly screamed
trying to change our nightmares
into dreams

The sun has come
the mists have gone
we see in the distance
our long way home

I was yours to have
and you were always mine
we loved each other
in and out, in and out, in and out of time.

13

Advocacy versus Accountability

In 2008, Maya supported her good friend Hillary Clinton for the Democratic presidential nomination. Her friendship with the Clintons stretched back decades. When Hillary lost, Maya switched her allegiance to Barack Obama.

That summer Obama gave his acceptance speech in Denver on the anniversary of the March on Washington. I'd known the senator for years. I had interviewed him a half dozen times. I had great respect for his intellect. I was also personally fond of him. When he secured the nomination, I was impressed with his political acumen and treated him as I treat all candidates: I pressed him on all the critical issues.

In the same manner, I had pressed George H. W. Bush, Bill Clinton, and George W. Bush. I saw it as my responsibility to fairly but closely question public servants.

Given my commitment to the legacy of Dr. King—a legacy that Obama himself purported to honor—I thought it only fitting that I probe the candidate's views on those issues closest to MLK's heart: racism, poverty, and militarism.

Because Obama was the first black to be nominated for the highest office in the land, many black voters understandably took great pride in his presence on the national stage. This was a huge historic moment. Beyond being proud, his black supporters also resented anyone who dared to do what I did—look deeply at his positions on the issues that would affect black people.

Two years earlier I had edited and published *The Covenant with Black America,* the first number one bestseller from a black publisher, which set out a plan of action to address the primary concerns of African Americans. In my commentaries about the candidates—John McCain as well as Barack Obama—I asked tough questions about whether either man was willing to specifically address those concerns.

Many in the black community—as well as those actively working in Obama's camp—thought I should give the junior senator from Illinois a pass. My reaction was that now, more than ever, he needed to address the issues spelled out in *The Covenant*. He had to be held accountable.

The pressure came quickly. Charles Ogletree called me to say that my scrutiny was hurting Obama's candidacy. As a professor of law at Harvard, Ogletree had taught both Barack and Michelle and had subsequently become a personal adviser to the candidate. Other high-ranking officials in Obama's campaign contacted me and said the same thing. In essence, they were asking me to back off. To every caller, my reply was the same.

"I'm doing my job," I said. "No more, no less."

When their exhortations didn't work, they played their trump card.

They asked Maya to call me.

It was a Saturday afternoon, and I was home in Los Angeles. Maya was calling from North Carolina.

"How are you, son?" she asked with more strength in her voice than I had heard in a long time.

"Doing well, Mother Maya. Great to hear from you. Great to hear you sounding strong."

"I've been listening to your commentaries, Tavis. As always, I listen to them with pride."

"Thank you."

"But recently my pride has been tinged with a bit of alarm."

"Over what?"

"Your treatment of Barack Obama."

I took a deep breath. I knew what was coming.

"You don't think I've been fair?" I asked.

"I think this is an extraordinary moment, Tavis. We have a chance to do something that, in my lifetime, I could never have imagined. We have a chance to elect a black man—a bright, highly educated, eloquent, good-hearted, and visionary black man—to be president of the United States. Do you appreciate this moment?"

"I do."

"Then don't you think we should be doing everything in our power to elect him?"

"I don't see that as my role."

"But isn't it your moral duty?"

"My moral duty is to fulfill my role. And my role isn't to serve as an advocate for Obama. That said, I don't hate Obama. I just love our people. And I believe that Obama needs to be held accountable for articulating the issues that matter most to the people who are voiceless. He needs to speak out about how he would relieve poverty, address the evils of racism, and show how he would curb—not grow—the militarism that siphons off dollars for those most in need. He needs to be pressed on those critical questions."

"He needs to be elected, Tavis. And it's our job—"

"With all due respect, Maya, you may see it as your job as a private citizen. But as a public broadcaster I never have and never will endorse a candidate."

"But Tavis, you're giving ammunition to his opponents. There's no reason not to soften your tone and dial back your criticism."

"There's every reason in the world, the most important being that I'd be abandoning a solemn oath to guard the public interest."

"Look, baby," said Maya, "all this lofty talk aside, I can't believe you have the slightest intention of voting for John McCain and Sarah Palin."

She knew me. "Of course I don't. But that's beside the point. That's a private matter, Maya. Just because I intend to vote for Obama and Biden doesn't mean that as a broadcaster I can treat them with kid gloves. I believe that Obama is worthy of being supported because his election just might open a path to progressive possibilities. But that doesn't mean I shouldn't press him to spell out programs that will affect the citizens in this country who lack political power."

"Do you really believe that McCain will do more for the poor than Obama?"

"No, I don't think McCain will do better. But I'm afraid that's still not the point. As a private citizen, you vote for the man who most closely reflects your values. But as a broadcaster, you closely examine *all* candidates. It's just that simple."

"Would that it were."

"But it is. It's great that you passionately and sincerely want this man to win. I'm glad you're campaigning. You've obviously been energized by his candidacy—and that makes me glad. I know how you feel, Maya. His election would be a symbol, and it would resonate around the world and down through history. I deeply appreciate that. But I also am asking you to appreciate that I have a job to do. I take that job seriously."

There was a long pause before Maya replied.

"Well, son," she said, "I suppose I should congratulate you for your seriousness."

"No, I should congratulate you, Maya, for your impassioned loyalty to the Democratic candidate. I applaud that."

"And, with some deep reservations, I must also applaud your principles. But if it's a close election, and this brilliant brother loses, you will be quick to hear from me."

"And as always," I added, "I will be delighted to hear from Mother Maya."

"Will you grant me one last word, Tavis?"

"Always."

"Lay off the guy, will you?"

I laughed and changed the subject. Maya never ended our conversations on anything less than a grace note, leaving me with the warm hug of her love.

14

Shower the People

It was 2011, and I drove to the great lecture hall with some trepidation. I knew that Maya had not been feeling well and had even considered canceling. She had been on the road for weeks, and the California trip, even in her custom bus, was a trek. When she phoned me from Arizona, her voice was noticeably weak.

"You sound a little tired," I said. "I'd love to see you, Mother, but perhaps you need to rest before trudging on."

"But, son," she said, "trudging on is what I do. It's what we all do. Do we have any alternative but trudging on?"

"Slowing down?"

"The psalmist said, 'Oh that I had wings like a dove! For then I would fly away, and be at rest.' But lacking the wings of a dove and the freedom of flight, I remain an earthbound traveler. The simple fact of moving forward brings me solace."

Her words brought *me* solace, and, in thinking about her frailty, I realized that once again Maya wasn't the one doing the worrying. I was.

Even though I arrived at the lecture hall early, I saw that all the seats were already filled. As she had done thousands of times before, Maya had sold out the place. The audience, largely female, could not have been more diverse—whites, blacks, Hispanics, and Asians, ranging in age from teenagers to the elderly. I could feel the eagerness with which they awaited Maya's arrival. I, too, was eager to see her.

I parked myself in the green room and was reading e-mail on my phone when the door opened. Maya was rolled in on a wheelchair, the respirator attached to her face. I was shocked. From the sound of her voice on the phone, I knew she was fragile, but I hadn't imagined her deterioration to be this dramatic. Her head was slightly slumped over and her arms were slack. She didn't see me. After she was situated in the room, I walked over.

"Is that you, young Tavis Smiley?" she asked with labored breath.

"Not so young, Mother Maya, but it's me."

"Bless your heart for coming out to see me. But if you don't mind, dear, I'm going to need a moment alone before I make my grand entrance."

"I completely understand," I said.

"Be sure and come by afterward."

I left the green room and made my way to my seat in the huge auditorium. I could feel the buzz. The audience couldn't wait to see Maya, but I couldn't help wondering—how in the world was she going to pull this off? It was inconceivable that the woman in the wheelchair I had just seen in the green room, a woman who appeared listless and weak, could take the stage and, of her own volition, command the audience's attention for more than a few minutes. Just the act of breathing was a chore. I wondered whether at the last minute she might cancel. And when it was ten, fifteen, and then twenty minutes past the starting time, my concern grew.

Finally, with the help of an aide, Dr. Maya Angelou walked to center stage and bowed before the standing ovation that greeted her. Her walk was certain, calm, and deliberate. Her respirator was nowhere to be found. Neither was there a hint of hesitation as she waved confidently to her admirers before taking a seat in a simple armchair.

"I greet you with great gratitude," she said. "My sisters, my brothers, my daughters, my sons, I greet you in love."

Then the miracle happened. The woman in the wheelchair was transformed into a woman in motion—not physical motion but linguistic motion. Spiritual motion. She transformed what had seemed an exhausted energy into a spirit of inexhaustible enthusiasm. She came to life and was the Maya I first knew decades before in Ghana. She was perky. She was alert. She was perceptive. She was charming. She was funny. She told anecdotes about her grandmother, her mother, her friendships with illustrious figures, her friendships with everyday people, her struggles as a young single mother, her failures, her triumphs, her strategies for survival, her love of cooking and progressive politics and the sonnets of Shakespeare and the singing of Abbey Lincoln and the verse of Langston Hughes and the prose of Toni Morrison and the acting of Roscoe Lee Browne and the scholarship of W. E. B. Du Bois. She read excerpts from her memoirs; she read from her poetry. And although she didn't dance, she described her days as a dancer with such thrilling expression and artful gesticulation that it was almost as if she rose up out of her chair and became Miss Calypso all over again. Her spirit was in motion. Her words had wings. It was a beautiful performance, an openhearted and stirring theatrical event in which she received and extended boundless love. If you arrived feeling blue, she chased those blues away. If you arrived feeling good, you left feeling better. And yes, at the end, she spontaneously broke into a hymn of hope, the one about going to the valley though not to stay, but then her soul got happy and she stayed all day.

The crowd would have stayed with her all night. They were up on their feet, singing along, giving her a roaring ovation that wouldn't stop.

Maya remained in the chair and waved, her eyes wet with tears. Her admirers waved back, many of them in tears as well.

Afterward I went back to the green room to congratulate her on her triumph. The place was jam-packed. I spotted her in a corner. She was back in her wheelchair and back on her respirator. She spotted me and motioned me over. When I approached her, she extended her hand. I took her hand, bent over to kiss her on the cheek, and whispered in her ear, "You killed."

She broke into a broad smile.

"Oh, Tavis," she said, her voice filled with excitement, "isn't it glorious to be alive?"

I kept it together until I got into my car and turned on the CD player. I had slipped in a James Taylor disk. As I drove off, James sang, "Shower the people you love with love, show them the way that you feel."

I didn't get far. I had to pull over.

I had witnessed a shower, a miraculous revival.

"They say in every life, they say the rain must fall," sang James. "Make it rain."

Maya had brought on the rain.

Over the next few years my life got busy, but no busier than Maya's. She continued to write books, and, with every new publication, she came on my television or radio show as a guest. I never let four or five months go by without visiting her home in Winston-Salem or Harlem.

It was impossible not to notice her physical deterioration. And it was also tough not to worry for her health—I had for years. But in Maya's presence, I acted as though nothing was wrong. It was easy to put my worry to the side for a little while because, intellectually and spiritually, nothing *was* wrong. The good cheer, the endless optimism, the keen interest in others, the planning of future projects, the talking, the cooking, the high-spirited games of Word Crunch—Maya was indefatigable.

Then on May 28, 2014, I was in New York City. The next day I was scheduled to speak at a national book convention, where I was to introduce my study of the last year in the life of Martin Luther King Jr., *Death of a King*, a subject that I had discussed with Maya on countless occasions. I was in my hotel room, going over notes, when the text messages and e-mails came flooding in: Maya had died at her home in Winston-Salem. She was eighty-six.

I looked out the window. Twenty floors below, people were walking the streets of the city as they always walk the streets of the city. Cars and taxis hurried by as they always hurried by. Life went on as life always goes on.

That didn't seem right.

People should stop walking. Cars and taxis should pull over. The world should stop turning. Without Maya, the world was without its animation, its meaning and rhythm. The world, suddenly, was not the same.

My friend was gone.

I knew that the pain in my heart and the tears in my eyes were shared by millions of her admirers. I knew that the great body of her work was eternal. Her love was eternal. She had enjoyed a fruitful and even glorious longevity. There was reason to celebrate. And yet living life without being able to call Maya and hear her reassuring voice was a dark and lonely prospect.

The next morning I went to the podium to address the convention. My heart was heavy, but I held my head high. I said, "We are all who we are because somebody loved us. None of us walks this journey alone. We are inextricably linked to the love and service of others. This moment is a bit surreal for me, because yesterday we lost

Dr. Maya Angelou. I am who I am because of the love Dr. Angelou showed me, a love that she showed so many over a lifetime of love. Ironically, she was born on the same day of the year—April fourth—that Dr. King was killed. Maya attended Dr. King's funeral, as well as the funeral of Malcolm X. That was Maya. She bridged the differences; she brought together the factions; she spoke the language of universal acceptance and compassion. When I was a young boy, it was the poetry of Maya Angelou that opened my eyes to the beauty of language. It was Maya who showed me how art can be transformative. It was the poem that said in its thrilling conclusion:

Out of the huts of history's shame
I rise
Up from a past that's rooted in pain
I rise
I'm a black ocean, leaping and wide,
Welling and swelling I bear in the tide.

Leaving behind nights of terror and fear
I rise
Into a daybreak that's wondrously clear
I rise
Bringing the gifts that my ancestors gave,
I am the dream and the hope of the slave.

I rise

I rise

I rise."

That night I flew home to Los Angeles with Maya owning my mind. Planes were still flying through the night as though nothing had changed. I still couldn't process it. I still couldn't fathom the loss.

For a few minutes I closed my eyes and remembered my last time with Maya. It was at her home in Winston-Salem only a few months before. We were sitting in the kitchen. It seemed like all our deepest discussions took place in Maya's beloved kitchen. It was late in the afternoon, the moment Frankie Beverly calls "the golden time of day." Earlier we had watched a Joel Osteen television presentation that was filled with encouragement and optimism.

"I love this man," said Maya. "He has a light about him. There is a light in his eyes and goodness in his words."

I agreed.

We marveled at the way certain preachers were able to escape the narrow confines of doctrinaire theology and touch the hearts of people who might not even consider themselves religious.

"You're one of those preachers," I said.

"Hardly," Maya said with a laugh. "I would not have made a good minister. I'm too willing to live with unanswered questions."

After tea and cookies, somehow we returned to our long-running debate—which is greater, love or courage?

"I thought I answered that question long ago, dear Tavis. But I see that my answer wasn't satisfactory to you."

"I just don't see putting anything above love," I said.

"It's not about above or below. It has to do with the righteous order of things."

"How so?" I asked her. She sat back and took a few breaths.

"Let's take this thorny question of death. For every natural reason, that question has been on my mind. And though I have said time and again that I do not fear death, it surely weighs on me. The idea of losing one's consciousness, as we understand consciousness, is a profound prospect. One wonders. One waits. It is easy to say that love protects me from the fear of death. But I contend that such a statement is glib. I cannot make that statement, Tavis. I really can't. I face the certain prospect of my demise with peace of mind because I have found courage—courage to open unknown doors, courage to walk through doors, and courage to explore new places. It is courage that allows me to consider the final mystery not with apprehension but with genuine curiosity—and even excitement."

"But how, Maya, did you ever attain that courage?"

She paused before answering. The sun was setting. The kitchen was bathed in a cooling twilight. Maya's voice was tired. She relied on her respirator for breath and clasped her hands in front of her. But despite the fatigue and strain, there was strength in her answer to my question.

"The search for courage," she said, "is one of life's great adventures. I've been living that adventure since I was a little girl. I revel in the adventure. I cherish the adventure.

"I don't know how I knew this, Tavis, but in the deepest part of my soul I understood that the adventure itself required courage. And because I didn't want to miss out on the fun—I didn't want to deny myself the sheer joy of going through this human form, with all its heartaches and joys—I simply did what was required. I mustered the courage to forge ahead. Because of that, I have lived the life that I wanted to live. And so can you, Tavis. So can everyone."

Epilogue

A few weeks after her passing, Maya came to me in a dream. I can't recall the details; I can only recall her powerful presence. I was deeply moved and felt compelled to reach out to her. I got up, walked to my study, and wrote this letter:

Dear Maya,

I know I'm not your only child. You had thousands of children. All I know is that I'm fortunate enough to have been allowed in your space. Your space was always open and loving, warm and welcoming, nurturing and affirming.

What a blessing!

Given where my life started, never in my wildest dreams could I have imagined even meeting you, much less being embraced by you. I want to say that I don't feel worthy, but I know my words would offend you. You'd stop me midsentence.

I want to thank you for so many things.

You were my cosmic connection to everyone I wished I had known—Du Bois, Baldwin, Nina Simone—not to mention Malcolm, Martin, Mandela. These were all your friends. But Maya, you also included me in your world. I still can't believe it.

So thank you for opening your heart and your home. You let me be me in your presence. Without judgment. For a young black man trying to find his voice and make his way in the world, that's a precious gift. You let me interrogate you, challenge you, question your authority—and all in the name of love.

If it's true that we are who we are because somebody loved us, I am who I am because you loved me.

I now know that before the foundation of the world, almighty God devised and declared our meeting and abiding friendship. The divine arrangement was in place. You were a beacon of light and hope helping to guide my life.

"Baby," you told me, "we find our path by walking it."

Well, Maya, I'll keep walking until we meet again.

Acknowledgments

My work and witness is most often jazzlike. That is to say, I'm part of an ensemble, which features a brilliant collaborator, David Ritz, and a wonderful researcher, Jared Hernandez. To the extent you find the music we make pleasing, I thank these gentlemen for making me sound good.

To the rest of the band, I am deeply grateful: Reagan Arthur, John Parsley, Malin von Euler-Hogan, Liz Garriga, Victoria Chow, Kimberly McFarland, and David Vigliano.

Let's keep making music that moves and motivates!

Finally, my deepest appreciation to the family of Maya Angelou and her personal staff for always being so kind to me over the course of many years: Guy Johnson, Colin Johnson, Fran Berry, Patricia Casey, Bettie Clay, Marlo Smith, and Lydia Stuckey.

—Tavis Smiley

With great gratitude to Tavis, for his faith in our collaboration; Jared, for superb research; John Parsley, David Vigliano, Malin von Euler-Hogan; and, as always, to my wife, Roberta, and my family—Alison, Jessica, Jim, Henry, Charlotte, Alden, James, Isaac, Elizabeth, and Esther; and dear friends—Harry Weinger, Alan Eisenstock, Herb Powell, John Tayloe, and Patrick Henderson.

—David Ritz

About the Authors

Tavis Smiley is the host and managing editor of *Tavis Smiley* on PBS and *The Tavis Smiley Show* from Public Radio International (PRI). He is also the bestselling author of seventeen books. Smiley lives in Los Angeles.

David Ritz, who collaborated with Smiley on *Death of a King* and *What I Know for Sure*, has worked with everyone from Ray Charles and Marvin Gaye to Aretha Franklin and B.B. King.